A Backse
from the Phantom

A Backseat View from the Phantom

A Memoir of a Marine Radar Intercept Officer in Vietnam

Fleet S. Lentz, Jr.,
Col USMCR (Ret)

McFarland & Company, Inc., Publishers

Jefferson, North Carolina

LIBRARY OF CONGRESS CATALOGUING-IN-PUBLICATION DATA

Names: Lentz, Fleet S., Jr., 1946– author.
Title: A backseat view from the Phantom : a memoir of a Marine radar
intercept officer in Vietnam / Fleet S. Lentz, Jr., Col USMC (Ret).
Other titles: Memoir of a Marine radar intercept officer in Vietnam
Description: Jefferson, North Carolina : McFarland & Company, Inc.,
Publishers, 2020 | Includes bibliographical references and index.
Identifiers: LCCN 2020022086 | ISBN 9781476682075 (paperback) ∞
ISBN 9781476640808 (ebook)
Subjects: LCSH: Lentz, Fleet S., Jr., 1946– | Vietnam War,
1961–1975—Aerial operations, American. | Vietnam War,
1961–1975—Campaigns—Vietnam. | United States. Marine Fighter
Attack Squadron 115—Military life. | Vietnam War, 1961–1975—
Personal narratives, American. | Phantom II (Jet fighter plane) |
Air pilots, Military—United States—Biography. | Nam Phong Royal
Thai Air Force Base.
Classification: LCC DS558.8 .L46 2020 | DDC 959.704/34092 [B]—dc23
LC record available at https://lccn.loc.gov/2020022086

BRITISH LIBRARY CATALOGUING DATA ARE AVAILABLE

ISBN (print) 978-1-4766-8207-5
ISBN (ebook) 978-1-4766-4080-8

Front cover: F-4 Phantom from Marine Fighter Attack Squadron 115
(VMFA-115)

Printed in the United States of America

*McFarland & Company, Inc., Publishers
Box 611, Jefferson, North Carolina 28640
www.mcfarlandpub.com*

For my children—
Leah, Drew, Peter, Kerry and Kevin—
and my grandchildren

Table of Contents

Table of Contents

Acknowledgments

This must start with my wife Kathy Crawley. She has done much of the heavy lifting on this effort and without her encouragement, correcting, organizing and other hard work, it would not have happened.

Going further back, I give Mr. John Alexander Graves III, Capt, USMC, and Saipan veteran, a hand salute. Mr. Graves was an esteemed friend and writer who told me I had a voice. He sits on my shoulder even now. To his inestimable wife Jane Cole Graves, I give a hug and kiss. Both John and Jane read this work in its roughest phase and urged me to keep writing anyway. From Jane I learned a writing formula that stays with me yet.

This book would not have happened without all enlisted men who served in VMFA-115 in 1972–1973. They kept me alive. Hats off to them, sincere appreciation and admiration.

To the staff of the *VMFA-115 1972–1973 Silver Eagles Cruise Book*. The book lists its editorial staff, Lt. B.E. Poley, SSgt. T.R. Davidson, and Sgt. J.L. Long; primary photographers, Lt. Poley, SSgt. Davidson; and other photographers, Capt. M.M. Johnson, SSgt. J.E. Baker, Sgt. R.S. Erbs, Sgt. R.K. Gunnel, Sgt. J.W. Tisch, Cpl. J.E. Stone. I don't know which photographer took specific pictures I have used from the cruise book, so I give to all these Silver Eagles a nod of thanks for the pictures, for helping to capture all the memories of that year and for information used as the basis for much of the VMFA-115 history included in this work.

A nod of appreciation to Dr. Fred (Mule) Allison, Maj, USMC (Ret), Historian, U.S. Marine Corps History Division, a good Cowboy RIO, and to his staff at the Division for their support and help.

Special gratitude to my Marine friends J.D. Howell, LtGen, USMC (Ret), who fielded a lot of bothersome questions and always answered straightly, and to Alvin F. Marshal, Jr., Maj, USMC (Ret), who did the same.

As well, to Marines Dale Anderson, John Basci, Jack P. Brown, Matt Campbell, W.T. Hicock, Rich Krsiean, Mike Overstreet, James W. Piggott, C.C. Rice, J.E. Rice, W.W. Round, Gregory D. Taylor, Mike Whitted, and

Acknowledgments

to Jim Sluder, MajGen, USAFR (Ret). Thanks to Joe Rice, in particular, for reading the manuscript in its final stages.

Knowing nods to Henry Curtis Ivy, Col, USMC (Ret); Aubrey W. Talbert, Col, USMC (Ret); Fred Schober, LtCol, USMC, and W.J. Simpson, Maj, USMC. May they rest in peace.

Thanks to Minrose Gwin and Amy Beeder, two stalwart friends and teachers from the University of New Mexico's Taos Writers Conference, which I attended several times in the early 2000s. I was their worst student.

To my special civilian friends, starting with Susan Yarbrough, long a dear friend and a good critic; Tom Bond, early reader of a very rough manuscript; Nathan Cone of Texas Public Radio, and Coleen Grissom of Trinity University, both of whom unknowingly breathed life into this effort at just the right time; Barry and Anne Mahoney for critiquing early drafts and supporting me in many other ways; and Wayne Gelfand, an early-early reader. To Carol Cowden, Amanda McBroom, Scott Downing, Robert Hinds and C.A. Hinojosa III of Mercedes, Texas. In different ways they nurtured my love of writing at various stages along the way.

To Roxanne M. Kaufman, Marine Corps Aviation Association Director of Operations and editor of *Yellow Sheet* and *MCAA Journal,* where an early version of "The Ten-Degree Run" was published in May 2017.

And to my oldest son Drew, who asked the questions that started this memoir. Thanks, man.

Preface

This book is my memoir of one calendar year, September 1972 to September 1973, when I served a tour in the Southeast Asia campaign as a young Marine aircrewman, new to war. Based at the Royal Thai Air Force Base in Nam Phong, Thailand, we called it The Rose Garden. My year coincided with the official end of the war in Vietnam in January 1973 but also included combat flying in Laos and Cambodia after that official end in Vietnam. By late September 1973, it was all finally over. I returned to the world.

No one, to my knowledge, has written of the Marine aviation effort during those final months. I wanted to record my experience, our experience, so that what we did there under the orders of our government and out of whatever sense we had of patriotism or duty would not fall through the cracks of history.

In the fine recent documentary *The Vietnam War: A Film by Ken Burns and Lynn Novick*, which touched briefly on the war's end, the Marines at The Rose Garden were not mentioned. The Marine aviation effort in those months was not mentioned at all. It became clear to me that my part of the war was unknown, almost forgotten. But good men flew there, some died there, and their contributions deserve acknowledgment.

The book is personal. It is not about politics or really even about big-picture history. We had neither time nor resources to keep up with what was going on politically. As the year unfolded, our news source was the *Stars and Stripes* newspaper, which was a week old when we got it, if we got it. But we knew our missions and executed them, living hop to hop.

It is not an academic work. I do not include notes or a bibliography. I have read widely about military history and Marine history, though, and have included (Appendix G) a short list of some of the books that have been interesting or important to me and have no doubt influenced my perspective.

I write as a Marine with a 31-year tenure, which I ended with the rank of colonel. The book is about Marines, my job as a radar intercept officer (RIO), and our daily lives, including what we did to stay human. The book

1

roughly follows this order: Entry into my new world, breaking in, notable combat hops and times, comments on secondary jobs we all held, my transfer to a higher echelon while still stationed in The Rose Garden, the retrograde or pullout, and noteworthy people and times—some outlandish, some somber. In the final chapter and epilogue, I reflect on lessons that I learned from my combat experience and on two trips back to Vietnam long after my war year was finished. Perhaps those trips were when my processing of my war year really began.

I wrote primarily from memory, which has served me particularly well. I have always had a decent ability to remember detail. While I was in Thailand in 1972–1973, my only writing was letters home to family and friends. There were no journals to draw from. In writing this book my best resource material included consultations with my own Aviator's Flight Logs, the *VMFA-115 1972–1973 Silver Eagles Cruise Book* (much like a high school yearbook), queries to the U.S. Marine Corps Historical Division, and numerous conversations with other men who were also stationed at The Rose Garden during my year. Many of them I am still in touch with today.

Of course, my memory has occasional glitches. I have done my best to be accurate. I regret any mistakes or omissions. They are my own and unintentional.

My memoir is definitely a work of nonfiction but I have chosen to write it using, in some instances, the style of the story-teller, including dialogue, indicated by quotation marks. The situations, though certainly based on my own impressions, are as accurate as I can make them and the dialogue is probably pretty accurate as well. Though I can't guarantee it is 100 percent accurate, I can guarantee that it conveys the gist, tone and spirit as much as almost 50 years' distance allows. I've used italics liberally not only for emphasis but also to denote military slang and written and thought remembrances, as opposed to the spoken dialogue.

I have referred to the people in this memoir not by name but by title, callsign or nickname. Some of the callsigns are real; some, I made up. The people mentioned will know who they are but their identities are protected, whether they really need to be or not.

I have several audiences. Of course, my fellow Marines and other Vietnam-era combatants. Their friends and families who may want to know more than they currently do about what happened *over there*. Readers interested in this often-troubling era in our country's history. And the broader audience who simply may like good stories, tinged with both darkness and humor. I've tried to define and explain with the non-military audiences in mind without being condescending to my military audience. The appendices are included in that spirit.

The people stationed at The Rose Garden were young Marines living and flying together in high stress situations. Without being gratuitous, I sometimes use the language, including the profanity and what I see now as sexist language, that we used then. Not to do so seemed to me to be inauthentic. I hope the language is not too offensive to the reader.

That year was a long time ago but it lives on. Seems like last week.

Semper Fidelis.

Prologue:
What Did You *Really* Do
in the War, Dad?

September 2008

I was having a beer with my oldest son Drew one Sunday afternoon about ten years ago. We were sitting outside under the live oaks in my Texas backyard when my cell phone showed a call from a Tennessee number. I hadn't heard from this guy in a while so I told Drew I'd just be a minute or two and walked off to take the call. When I returned, I said the name of the caller. "The Fat Maggot," he said, as if on cue. He laughed. "The Fat Maggot!"

The caller had indeed been a friend I called The Fat Maggot, a fellow former Marine officer who had gone through Officer Candidate School, OCS, and pre-flight training with me and had served with me stateside flying F-4s before we both went overseas.

Flying in the Vietnam war out of Da Nang, Vietnam, and Nam Phong, Thailand, I had flown on his wing on my first combat mission, or hop. The Fat Maggot and I also shared the same close quarters with three other young men for most of a year. Forty-one years later, just a month before the phone call, I had transacted commercial aviation business with him.

Andrew became uncharacteristically quiet and looked away, as if puzzling, studying something. "Pops," he said, "you know, all my life I've heard talk about the F-4, the Marine Corps, Vietnam, Top Gun and other stuff. All the stories about how you guys liked to set your hair on fire, what you all used to do. And here we are in Texas on a Sunday afternoon. You're way out of the Marine Corps, don't fly F-4s anymore, and you are now talking with this guy forty years later. I wasn't even born when you met The Fat Maggot!"

And then he got to the real question. "Dad, what did you *really* do in Vietnam? I wanna know. What did you do that makes you guys keep up, stay

5

in touch? What's with that?" Now *I* was puzzling. Drew was serious, as serious as I had ever seen him. He really wanted to know. I knew my son well, when he was fluffing me and when not. This was not fluffing.

In a quick answer to his question, I said that one thing I had learned was who to trust and why. TFM and I were in combat together. We lived in the same hootch in a shithole in the jungle. We got to know each other in ways most people don't.

Even though we weren't infantry Marines, we fought. The infantry war was much more visceral than our war in the air but we saw enough. Some of us didn't make it back. But those of us who did make it back picked up our lives and moved on, or tried to. The war was not something we forgot. Or maybe others could forget but I couldn't, didn't. Too much had happened.

We had been Marines in a war. We had been taught how to fight but we were also taught to not forget. I told Drew I could still remember my rifle number at OCS and my drill instructors' names and ranks. Damn near every Marine I knew remembered too. We all still knew the words to the Marine Corps Hymn and stood up when it was played, anywhere, anytime. I smiled as I said there was no such thing as an Ex-Marine. *Ex* means out of. All Marines no longer serving or wearing the uniform are *former* Marines. They are not *out of*. There is a tie that binds.

Besides, my war was more than one year with 131 combat hops and a bunch of secondary ground jobs. It was only one calendar year but it was also a compressed lifetime with its own before, during and after. That one year stretched into a career that ended up as 31 years, two months and 12 days of total time as a U.S. Marine. It spanned, will span my entire life. The men who shared that life with me were close to me in a way that is hard to explain.

I felt my mind choke down and stop. All this was way too much to answer Drew's question. All I could tell him then was that it was hard to explain. I felt a little condescending as I asked if he knew what a paradox was. "Yeah," he said, "I think so. It's like that line in the Eagles song 'Hotel California.' Something like *you can check out but can't ever leave.* Right?" "Right," I said. "My time in Vietnam was a paradox. It was the best time of my life and the worst time, all at the same time."

Off to the side of my stalled mind lurked the thought that this son—born five years after I got back from Vietnam—could not really know who his father was then. Even if I tried to tell him, he might not be able to get his mind around it all. I told him it would take a longer explanation than we had time for that day. Besides, he had to go home to his kids, my grandkids.

It would be better if I wrote him a letter about it. We shook hands, hugged and said goodbye.

***

As I thought more about his question, "Dad, what did you *really* do in Vietnam," I realized my answer could easily become the same sort of stumbling answer my own dad had given me about his service in World War II. Short factual sketches of people, ships, ports and the like. Which was not an answer. I wanted to tell as much as could be told, the good and the other.

It comes to me now that I wanted my better self to pass on objective information tinged with how *I* actually saw the experience. Or how it saw me. Talk to the kind of things that I had wanted to hear from my own dad. Like *were you scared*?

As I listened to my own brain whifferdill around, searching for a place to start my real answer to Drew's question, I remembered the older men who were veterans in my town when I was a kid. There were the World War I men who sold poppies on Armistice Day from a card table on the downtown sidewalk in front of the five-and-dime. My friends and I thought they were old geezers, doing what old geezers did. Then there were the World War II men. I later learned that one of those men was on Omaha Beach on D-Day. Another had earned a Silver Star in fierce infantry combat in Germany. My high school football coach was in the Battle of the Bulge where he contracted trench foot.

Most of these men from both wars had probably not told their stories to their own sons. I know now that some things from a war are best left untold. I also know of the later sadness of sons and daughters whose fathers never shared their stories. But those are not my sons and daughters. My hope is that my own children and some unknown sons and daughters besides my own may learn something of their own old man from this effort. Drew asked what I did in the war and I will try to answer. Vietnam may be an asterisk in American history but not to me. It was my time, my war.

***

If each examined life has a *golden* time when life is intensely lived, when the future seems endless and dreams seem achievable, that time for me was September 1972–September 1973. My senses were wide open, while at the same time fast death was just a millisecond away.

My golden time was alloyed with steel, titanium and tin. That golden time smelled like jet fuel, burnt charcoal and raw human shit. It was a time

7

enclosed in nylon mesh, under a canvas roof, then a tin roof, then a Lexan canopy, while I listened at night to Judy Collins. I was surrounded by some of the best enlisted and officers any U.S. Marine Corps will ever have. We served at Da Nang, Vietnam, and Royal Thai Air Force Base, RTAFB, Nam Phong, Thailand. To those who lived and died there, Nam Phong was The Rose Garden.

SECTION ONE

My New World

CHAPTER 1

Going Down

September 1972

In September 1972, I received my port call and learned when and how I would make the trip from the U.S. to Vietnam. I had been an officer in the Marine Corps with a Reserve Commission for two years and nine months. I had made a commitment to the Marine Corps for six years' active duty. I had worn my wings one year and eight months and had a meager 270.8 hours in the F-4 Phantom II jet. I was a Radar Intercept Officer, or RIO, a back-seater. I ran the plane's radar, did most of the communication, and navigated.

I finally took off from Marine Corps Air Station, MCAS, Iwakuni, Japan, after a week there en route. Iwakuni was 1st Marine Aircraft Wing Headquarters and every aircrew departed for Vietnam from there. I was a replacement Marine RIO, a passenger on an Air Force C-141 cargo plane. We took off late in the afternoon and I was in for an all-night flight to Nam Phong, Thailand, with a stop in Vietnam.

I had just had a nervous drink with a major at the Officers Club, or O-Club, bar in Iwakuni, which was weird because first lieutenants usually didn't socialize with Heavies, or field grade officers, majors and up. But the Heavy had asked me where I was headed. I told him Nam Phong, the jungle. He had just been there, he said, and was "too old for that Boy Scout shit." I had no idea who the man was.

I figured I would be awake all the way to Thailand. My head was too full for me to have any real rest. Boarding the plane, I recalled the last thing my drill instructor, or DI, had told us at OCS. Just before he couldn't talk to us like a DI anymore. He had been a member of the First Battalion, Ninth Marines, The Walking Dead, and he knew Vietnam as did few others. We were minutes away from being commissioned when he said, "Listen up, ladies. Only the good die young, so be the worst possible son of a bitch you can be." On the plane, I wished he could see me. I had earned my first lieutenant bars. I was on my way to my first and only shooting war.

Section One—My New World

The other replacement Marine aircrew aboard that plane were probably thinking about the same things I was. Each stayed quiet. Whatever personal thoughts we had were drowned in and walled off by engine noise. It had turned real. The Big It. Finally, I was going. One way down, no way out.

Vague preconceptions rolled and surfaced, flipped and dove again in my mind. Reminded me of the oxygen-starved gar and carp I had seen in the muddy, flooding Rio Grande River near my home in South Texas. Dark, vague apprehensions solidified into cold lumps in my gut, materializing later as a checklist in my mind. I had actually made a written checklist and gone over it almost obsessively every day. The list ran the gamut from will to wife, to parents and family, to friends male and female. All the while the words to Peter, Paul & Mary's version of the popular song "Leaving on a Jet Plane" kept running through my head.

On the flight, I oddly found my first thoughts focused on my mother. I had known of older men, minutes away from death, whose words to their mothers were the last sounds made in their lives. I really did not want that. I decided to talk to her in the silence of my mind before I came to the end.

Before I went to Vietnam, my mother wasn't concerned with politics or war. She was busy trying to make ends meet. She wanted and worked to be the best wife and mother she could be. I had a younger brother and sister who were still college kids. As show time approached for me, my mom had gone so far as to suggest that I could teach school *or something*, as she cryptically put it. Her hinting referred to people we knew who suddenly had an old football injury flare up with a doctor's note for draft deferment. One friend of the family had fled to Canada and countless others married hurriedly and impregnated their young wives because fathers, if drafted at all, were drafted later. I was 1-A and she knew it.

My mother was a woman whose husband, my dad, served all of World War II plus six months afterward. Her uncles had fought in World War I and her grandfather had fought in the Civil War. He was shot and captured, imprisoned in New Orleans until after Appomattox.

This war, though, was different. *I* was her *son*. Her reluctance, her unwillingness to speak openly about her fears reminded me how sick the country was of the Vietnam war. With the loud drone of the plane all around me, I spoke silently to her. I told her I loved her.

I thought about how joining the Marine Corps, becoming commissioned, completing flight school and getting wings were sources of upheaval, controversy and unrest in my three-year marriage. I remembered my then-wife, who was expected by the Marine Corps of that time to participate in what seemed to her inane tasks, saying to me one day, *Who joined the Marines? You did. I didn't.* But I had done the right things, having a pay allotment sent to her and making her the beneficiary of death benefits, complete with a paid-for funeral.

Even with Mickey-Mouse ears, the sound suppressors we had been issued to drown out engine noise, it was still too loud to sleep. Plus the noise was coming from inside my head. I had time, too much random time. Fatigue-tinged thoughts started taking over. I found myself trying to make sense of how I had gotten here. I began backtracking.

***

I had always thought of my life as common as any life there ever was. I was decidedly a small town, rurally oriented kid who always watched where his feet were going. The trail or road I was following kept my attention in one way or another. Looking back mentally while in that plane, I saw many paths of broken arcs, pieces of paths, some that were connect-the-dots routes, all leading here.

I remembered making my way to grade school in 1952, a barefooted, snot-nosed kid in Mercedes, Texas. That was the first path I remember following, wearing second-hand, dew-soaked, rolled-up blue jeans.

That path led to trails in the brush beside our house, where I followed rabbit runs. Paths at the Boy Scout summer camp I went to for six years. Trails our cows cut with sharp hooves between the corrals and the pasture in the brush where they grazed. The Lost Mine Trail at Big Bend National Park, where I had followed my dad. A high point of my life at age 14.

As I got older, the paths took turns and detours. They became less about what interested me and more about what other people thought I should do. Their suggestions became models I was imposing on my life—what I should think, what I should be, what I should want. Under the noise in my mind was the realization that all the paths had converged and were heading me to a place where I could actually die. At the young age of 26.

Several guys I had grown up with were long since dead from Vietnam. Death wasn't entirely new to me. I had already seen death, had been a part of high performance flying in which it was not unusual for people to die. I already knew it didn't necessarily take war to kill you in a jet fighter. And I knew that, regardless, I had signed up for this war, volunteered to live or die with it. But that clear logic was pretty damned cold comfort just then.

All that thinking, though, did not allow escape from the upcoming reality that this time, it was my own death I was contemplating, not someone else's. I had always thought that death happened to the other guy. This time I knew *I could be the other guy.* The very present aspect of my own death hovered a while and then just went away. I had known all along the possibility was there. But now, it was approaching *here.*

***

The food on board the C-141 consisted of C-Rations in olive-drab cans packed inside cardboard boxes. It was the usual bad, old *constipatory* stuff I was familiar with from field exercises at OCS and tent time at Cherry Point, N.C., my last peace-time station before going to war. Because we were on a plane, we couldn't light the fuel tabs used to heat the cans so we made do with cold, choke-butt cheese spread and hardtack chased with airplane water. No one was really interested in eating.

Eventually fatigue overcame it all—the questioning, regrets, memories, things left undone and unsaid. I lay down on the nylon-strapped red bench seats and passed out, with the Mickey-Mouse ears perpendicular to the line of fading vision.

CHAPTER 2

The Base

September 1972

A recruiting poster of those times showed a rabid Marine Drill Instructor with his mouth four inches from the ear of a boot recruit. The recruit flinches as the DI's spit flies. In bold print, the statement beneath read *We don't promise you a rose garden.*

On maps, the base was labeled the Royal Thai Air Force Base, Nam Phong, but those of us who lived there named the base where I would spend the next year for that same popular line from Marine Corps advertising *and* for Lynn Anderson's hit country-and-western song "Rose Garden."

Royal Thai Air Force Base, Nam Phong, was not an ideal base by any means but it was available to our government on short notice. President Nixon and his Secretary of State Henry Kissinger had recently decided to de-escalate the war. Among the first orders of business was the removal of Marines from Da Nang, Vietnam. A symbolic act. Combat flying wasn't wound down, only relocated to Nam Phong, where my outfit was sent in June 1972. Being Marines and ready to go anywhere, anytime, per the perpetual state of readiness Marines train to, we arrived in Nam Phong before our being stationed there had been fully thought through. So the order of the day was to improvise and then improvise again, then again. Go expeditionary.

We were Marines so that wasn't unexpected. The common wisdom was that Marines have done so much with so little for so long, we can now do everything with nothing. We did what we could. I should say *they* did. I didn't get to Nam Phong until September 1972. Even then the base was crude but it was better than the original deployees had to deal with.

The Rose Garden had begun as a CIA base, used for marshaling and transporting Southeast Asia allies into and out of theaters in that part of the world. It was strategically located about 25 miles west of the Mekong River, which separates Thailand from Laos and Vietnam. To the north, east and west of the base, the Thai jungle, regarded as an enemy avenue of

15

approach, regained control of the land. Guerrilla activity there was not unknown. Only on the south was there some open land where gently rolling country was broken up into small hand-farmed plots. Water buffalo roamed there and human manual laborers grew rice and tapioca.

The Garden was surrounded by *the wire*, more precisely, a high chain-link fence topped with razored concertina wire. The Marines based there and the Air Force who visited us were restricted to staying inside the wire unless we were on liberty, which came every two weeks. Of course, outside the wire there was nowhere to go for entertainment, no off-base town. Only miles of path-marked jungle.

Wooden guard towers stood every seventy yards inside the wire, each one armed with fixed machine guns, .50-calibers, positioned to form interlocking fields of fire. We were, after all, Marines and a war was still on. Thai soldiers, reinforced by U.S. Marine infantry, manned the towers. The base was theirs, not ours. There was no status of forces agreement with the Thai government at that time.

The Garden's focal point was a 10,000-foot-long airstrip that ran north-south through the base. It was built of concrete and pavement surrounded by dark red Thai clay and sand. When the visibility was good as we came in for a landing in the F-4, the airstrip appeared as a long hazy gash or a dirty flesh wound with a faint gray line down the middle. Most days visibility was poor, hazy. Some days the haze might be from WOXOF, meteorology-speak for Indefinite Ceiling, Sky Obscured. Or the haze could result from the indigenous Thai farmers burning jungle undergrowth in winter. Or maybe from boundary outflow from a front bringing in monsoonal weather. The monsoons blew sand and dirt ahead of them, sometimes for days. During the nine months of summer, the haze on the runway simply could be from the high relative humidity—90 percent—with imbedded thunderstorms. Not good flying weather. When the weather at the Garden was really bad, we would have to divert the jets to other Thai bases at Udorn, Ubon, Korat, or Takhli, Thailand. And on some hops, we stayed in Da Nang, Vietnam, where we refueled and rearmed routinely but no one wanted to overnight in Da Nang.

The air strip had two sets of arresting gear at either end, identical to an aircraft carrier's cross-deck arresting cables. Like the base, the airstrip wasn't ideal. The south end sloped downward at about five degrees. Landing a plane heavy with fuel or unexpended bombs could be dicey.

On either side of the air strip, mostly to the west, was the base proper. About 640 acres sloped westward downhill toward the jungle. The Garden

Typical hootches at The Rose Garden housed four to six men. Officer and enlisted hootches were the same but were separated by a clay-gravel road that ran between encampments of them. The author lived in the Maggot hootch with four other men, two with the callsigns Maggot and The Fat Maggot (*VMFA-115 1972–1973 Silver Eagles Cruise Book*).

was populated by 2,500 souls at any given time. We lived in tent-topped Southeast Asia huts called hootches in the Vietnam war vernacular. They were the best the Seabees could do on short notice.

Each hootch housed four to six Marines. Hootches for officers and enlisted were the same but they were separated by a graded clay-gravel road that ran between them. At various times the road was tarred but the monsoon rains beat the thinly poured tar into mud or dust after it dried. The tar, RC-600, never lasted very long.

The base had one medical dispensary, one brig or jail, one chow hall, one administrative headquarters, one chapel and thirty-odd six-hole outhouses, the well-known and oft visited shitters. There was no dependable running water. Electrical power was available as long as the diesel generators, supplied by a government contractor, were running. They were operative more than they failed but they failed often.

For an aircraft parking ramp surface, there was Marston matting, a slab of strengthened aluminum that interlocked and would blister a bare foot in

A gunny and two plane captains (L–R) truckin' in front of a Wonder Arch, one of three large, open-ended Quonset huts used as plane hangars at The Rose Garden. The men pictured were enlisted men responsible for launching and recovering aircraft (*VMFA-115 1972–1973 Silver Eagles Cruise Book*).

seconds. For hangars, we had three Wonder Arches, open-ended Quonset huts on steroids. For maintenance spaces, we had three three-story barns. Anyone with an agrarian background would have called them barns.

Forty-five or so aircraft were housed on the base—two CH-46 choppers for logistical support, one KC-130 tanker on rotational loan out of Okinawa, 28 to 30 F-4 Phantom IIs (B and J models) and 12 to 14 A-6 Intruder attack planes. We had no more than 12 jeeps in total. The grunts, or infantry, had a few big six-wheeled trucks. The MABSters from the Marine Air Base Squadron, or the gas and bombs guys who operated the bomb dump, also had a couple of six-bys.

***

Two smells dominated The Rose Garden, the ever-present smell of burnt jet fuel and the smell of untreated human feces. Burnt jet fuel had a familiar and almost pleasant toast-like smell. It was the smell of jet engines turning up, the smell of flying, of activity, of going and doing. The heavy, invasive smell of human excreta, on the other hand, was not so pleasant.

The hotter the weather, the more pungent both smells became and it was always hot. The coldest it got in winter was about sixty degrees Fahrenheit, hardly cold, but cold enough to put sleeping men under green wool army blankets. By noon, even after a chilly night, the temperature always made it back up to the nineties. Constant high humidity sharpened the smells, gave them depth. They went straight into the olfactory, no foreplay about it. These two smells stayed in the air as reminders of the primitive conditions we lived and flew in. Like the penetrating heat, they became familiar in their own way.

***

The base itself of that time and place has etched its way into my ordinary human mind. Memory of it comes back when I hear a certain popular song from then or when an e-mail appears in my in-box out of the blue from someone who was there. Remembering comes on the days the government has set aside as hallowed time to remember and honor those fallen in wars. Remembering is honoring, as I see it. The Garden was one of those places, which once lived in, cannot be forgotten. Men I knew died flying out of there. I do not want them forgotten.

On some days, the whole complex resembled an itinerant circus on the edge of a small town, mostly because everything was tented. We had our share of clowns, tigers, elephants, monkeys and high wire acts performed without a net. We also knew that at some point, the tents would be folded up and we would hit the road when the show was over. We were expeditionary. On other days, the complex could have been a prison. After all, it did house men who had killed and would kill again, who were locked in by razor wire and guards with automatic weapons.

Whatever it was, it was home to me for what seemed a very long time. It was a separate lifetime, a life sentence. With the pressure of combat operations and the unrelenting demands of flying high-performance jets, seconds augmented into minutes, minutes into hours, hours to days, weeks, months, years. When we took fire, seconds morphed into days.

Men who became my family lived in the Garden, too—brothers, uncles, cousins. In a way, the Garden resembled the home Robert Frost described in "The Death of the Hired Man" as "...the place where, when you have to go there, / They have to take you in." In that closeness, I shared with men personal things I never had told my own biological brother, much less my own father. Nor have I since. These men, my family. As the reels of an unedited movie unspool in my peace-time head, I call their names and those who died come to life.

Good men lived at The Rose Garden. Several were shot down, some were captured, some crashed, too many died. Others had children born to

19

them unseen in the faraway world. Marriages dissolved through the mail or began dissolving. Grandparents and parents passed away. Some men left at home infant children they would not watch grow up. While we were in Vietnam in 1972 and 1973, our lives at home went on relentlessly.

My time in the Garden was both pitch dark and full of humor that had light. I can say these many years later that I never felt as much fear and pain or laughed as hard and as honestly as I did then. I cried only once.

CHAPTER 3

Rules of the Road

September 1972

The grinding sound of the flaps and landing gear being lowered on the C-141 woke me up. I had only a minute to resurface and get back to the reality of time and place, both of which came fast. My government-issued watch showed it was around one in the afternoon. If the plane had stopped en route at Da Nang, I had slept through it.

The big cargo plane rolled onto the transient aircraft mat, shut down its inboard engines, dumped us and the mail sacks out and powered up to taxi down for takeoff, restarting the inboard engines on the taxi roll. The bird didn't even shut completely down to take on fuel. There was enough left for the pilot to get back to Da Nang or the Philippines. The Air Force over-nighted only at user-friendly bases, which The Rose Garden was not. That became evident soon enough.

Getting off the cargo plane, I spotted the tallest building at the end of the runway. The shortest control tower I had ever seen. As a standard fixture of any Naval or Marine airfield, Base Operations sat next to the tower. Both were of cheap expeditionary wooden construction. The control tower looked like one of the wooden water tanks on stilts I had seen in the Texas Valley as a kid. Or maybe like a deer blind. It could also have passed for a fishing shack on long wooden legs like those I had seen in Laguna Madre on the bayside of Padre Island. It was incongruous to see things in Nam Phong that looked like far South Texas.

I opened the screen door of the Base Ops porch and dumped my bags. A gunnery sergeant sat in the next room at an improvised plywood desk. "Which outfit do you have orders to ... *sir*?" he asked me in a bored voice, finally and reluctantly noting my rank insignia.

"Orders are for VMFA-115, Gunny. RIO." VMFA stands for Fixed-Wing Marine Fighter Attack but no one in the whole Marine Corps knows where the V came from. The Squadron number is 115, designated decades ago by the Department of the Navy. He stamped the receiving endorsement on the original orders and initialed them. "Welcome aboard … *sir*," he said with a sarcastic upturn at the end.

"Is there a phone anywhere I can use?" I asked him. He pulled a face on me that asked *Where do you think you are, boot?* as he reached down to the floor. He picked up a beaten, dusty khaki canvas bag trailing communications wire, or com wire. A crank and an antique-looking phone were sticking out of it. He gave the crank a few fast turns and after the switchboard answered, he handed the antique phone to me.

A male voice, a Marine in the communications section, said simply, "Operator." I asked to be switched to the admin section of VMFA-115 where an old friend from the OCS days now worked. "Wait one," the operator said and then I heard my friend answer. A familiar voice, finally.

Ten minutes later a jeep coughing red dust roared up and out stepped my friend. He had his standard shit-eating grin on his face, which conveyed *Hello dumbshit and welcome to hell!* He informed me straightaway that no one went by given names. Everyone used callsigns. His was The Fat Maggot. Only the Heavies used rank and last name and not even they did all of the time unless it was the CO, the skipper, or the XO, the number two. They called people whatever they wanted to.

***

I'm betting that callsigns have been around as long as there have been warriors. Native American tribes had a custom of war names, distinct from given names and often known only to other fighting men in the band or tribe. Marine fighter aviation's variant of this custom is the callsign, which without a doubt adds to its color and veracity. On one level, each squadron has its own callsign, assigned and registered officially by higher command somewhere. For instance, the VMFA-115 Silver Eagles squadron callsign is Blade. Since Vietnam, I have been in other squadrons with callsigns ranging from Linus to Gabe to Snake to Cowboy. Certain types of planes have callsigns too. For example, Marine refueling tankers use the callsign Basketball.

In most cases, peers or higher ups assign callsigns. We don't pick our own. In some cases, they just fit and make sense for the individual. Callsigns can come from anywhere. A physical feature. A personality trait. A play on words. A geographical reference. An identifying incident. A hard-to-live-down foul-up. Among those who would become my immediate circle at The Rose Garden, the callsigns are interesting, sometimes suggestive, sometimes not so much. *Agile, Bantam, Batjack, Beak, Branch, Bush Hog, Clipper, Cobra, Dog, Dog Style, Fish, Handsome, He Coon, Joker,*

Chapter 3. Rules of the Road

Mach-mach, Maddog, Maggot, Nacho, Pinko, Polly, Rat, Razor, Rock, Satan, Satin, Shadow, Slug Alpha, Spot, Square, Suitcase, The Fat Maggot, Tones, Watch Dog, Weasel, Yossarian, Zoobreath.

***

By the time I arrived at the Garden, each pilot and RIO also had his own individual callsign but this had not always been the case for RIOs. Around this time in naval aviation, RIOs were just coming into equality with pilots, full citizenship. Previously some pilots thought of RIOs as walking, talking, audio altimeters or 160-pounds of ballast. RIOs had put up with a lot of guff from pilots. Most of the time, it was friendly but sometimes it led to bar fights.

That all changed with the Navy F-4 crew from VF-96. In Vietnam earlier in 1972, this pilot and RIO had already *killed*, or shot down, four MiGs, the tough, lethal Russian- and Chinese-built fighter aircraft flown by the North Vietnamese Air Force. They were one *kill* away from shooting down five MiGs, or achieving Ace status, which would put them into superstardom. The RIO got all of that crew's first *tally-ho*'s. That is, he was the one who first sighted the MiGs they later shot down. Pilots, the *sticks*, had always prided themselves on doing that but after this RIO's accomplishments, they had to share that pride with RIOs, the *scopes*.

As a way to recognize our newly elevated status, RIOs decided the time had come for us to have our own callsigns. Before I went to Vietnam, when I was at Cherry Point, we had helped raise our status by formally listing RIOs' callsigns on the mimeographed index cards or kneeboard cards we carried as a reference in the cockpit.

As part of this process, I asked the senior RIO in our squadron what callsign he wanted for himself. He thought for a minute. "Coon," he said, "He Coon." When I looked at him quizzically, he explained he had grown up in backwoods Florida, near the Panhandle. The critter that ruled the woods in his growing up days was the he coon, and the senior RIO decided he himself would be a formidable He Coon. Later, Florida Governor Lawton Chiles adopted that moniker for the same reason. Little did I know that six months later, I would see He Coon at The Rose Garden. He had been my boss and became my friend. Still is.

***

I arrived in The Rose Garden without a callsign. My first name Fleet was unusual enough, if somewhat colorless. Many people didn't know it *was*

23

actually my real name. It sounded like it might be a callsign but some of the guys I had flown with at Cherry Point were at the Garden and had different ideas. One day after I started flying hops, I was scheduled to fly with a pilot whose callsign was Handsome. He pegged me as a nasally country hick, a grit, because I was from an agricultural background in Texas, chewed tobacco and rodeoed. Very soon, I became The Grit as in grits and gravy. But that wasn't enough. Handsome Latinized my callsign into Fleetius Grittus Maximus; he later added Ah Oom to the end of it. For gravity, he said. But in the air, gravity and elaboration gave way to brevity and I was just Grittus.

In airborne combat communications and relationships, brevity is essential and callsigns are brief. Grittus is both smartass and brief. What could be better?

**

When my friend picked me up at Base Ops, he began to fill me in. "I live in the Maggot hootch, where you'll be living," he said. "Next door to the Doghouse, the palace of a man with the callsign Dog."

"Around here just call me The Fat Maggot or TFM," he said as he shook my hand and helped me throw my gear in the jeep. "Can't just call me Maggot. There's already a Maggot. It's taken. He's a stick, lot of hops. He's good." That statement said everything, RIO to RIO, about that pilot.

I had known The Fat Maggot at Cherry Point, and the Maggot part of his callsign fit him rather well. He had always fought the system, gone his own way. Fat, however, was not an accurate description. TFM was six-feet-tall, right at 220 pounds, two-people wide. He had played college football as a tackle at the University of Richmond. Hardly a fat maggot except in outlook and sometimes behavior. He was wickedly intelligent in a quiet, almost academic way, though he camouflaged that well. His sense of humor was wry, smartly pointed, and he was always up to something, usually devilment.

TFM knew the drill. He got my paperwork squared away and walked me in to meet the Commanding Officer, or CO, a lieutenant colonel, callsign Clipper. "Welcome aboard, Fleet," Clipper said without any hi-howya-doin'-how-was-the-trip dressing. Clipper was short, wizened and beginning to bald. He seemed far older than his forty-something years. He was on his third combat tour and he knew the drill very well. I was fighting intense heat, fatigue and geographical vertigo at that moment, trying hard just to stay upright. He knew it, had seen it before.

**

Chapter 3. Rules of the Road

Before arriving at The Rose Garden, I had been lucky enough to get the scoop on Clipper from a friend whose callsign was Pinko. Prior to Clipper's tour at The Rose Garden, the VMFA-115 squadron, the Silver Eagles, had won awards. One of them was The Hanson Award for Marine Fighter Squadron of the Year, to be exact. In a mid-air collision in Da Nang, the squadron had lost its number two senior officer. Shortly thereafter, the old CO rotated back stateside. The experience had taken the heart of the squadron. For a while. Clipper was brought in as the CO. It was a tough time to be the new guy. Big shoes to fill, but fill those shoes he did.

Back at Cherry Point, Pinko and I had been in the worst squadron ever. We had flown together a lot, in F-4s and in his little privately-owned plane. He had told me I talked too much in the cockpit and he was right. He was an experienced old salt by the time he and I flew in combat together and I trusted him.

I believed Pinko when he said we had gone from the worst squadron to the best. He hadn't thought that anyone could get the Silver Eagles squadron back in fighting trim but Clipper had. "He's done a damned good job. He's one of those 'second lieutenants' who has a real healthy dislike for authority. He doesn't bend to anybody, whatever their rank." Pinko had paid Clipper a left-handed compliment. Calling a senior officer a second lieutenant meant his heart was in the right place. But that compliment might not get him very far career-wise. Pinko had gone on, "Clipper will take the hill in a fight and set his hair on fire when he's on liberty."

***

"TFM here will get you squared away," Clipper said. We jumped into the jeep and drove down the hill to the squadron's living spaces, boiling red dust all the way. As he ground the jeep into gear, TFM said, "I'm so fucking glad you are here. Now I can pass the SLJO job on to you." As the newest lieutenant aboard, I automatically became the Shitty Little Jobs Officer. At that time the SLJO billet, or assigned job, was coffee mess officer. I would be making the coffee till someone newer arrived.

TFM pulled the jeep up sharply at the company street, or the open space between two rows of hootches. "Gotta hump it from here, sixth hootch on the left. Already got you a cot and a rubber lady. You get a real rack, an actual bed, when the next guy rotates. It's up to you if you want a mosquito net. Some use 'em, some don't."

I lugged the bags down and put them in the hootch, hearing the sound of screen door springs open then slam shut behind me. The sound was familiar, another reminder of South Texas except that these doors were not

The 26-year-old author in front of his hootch six weeks after arriving at The Rose Garden, November 1972. He wrote on the back of this photograph, "Jungle Jim, the fighter RIO extraordinaire, in the uniform of the day, in front of hootch" (author's collection).

in the small mom-and-pop grocery stores in Mercedes. I tossed my things on my rubber lady, a black government-issued coffin-shaped air mattress. I was running dry on fuel in the heat and strangeness. TFM said, "C'mon, I'll give you the nickel tour while we have the jeep. Then I've got to give it back." He told me that only the skippers got jeeps. Everyone else drove Black Ferraris, or wore black boots, jungle or flight.

He took me to the hangar, which was not really a hangar. It was a tin-covered building that housed an open-air, makeshift ready room, operations office and any base maintenance efforts that needed to be kept dry. Electronics and radar. As he walked me through the barn, I met a few more individuals and promptly forgot their names. I was going out on my feet. He showed me the chow hall, one of two metal buildings on the base. We went to the Group Headquarters, where the senior officer sat, a full bird colonel. And last, to the admin hootches where our record books were kept and where we drew our pay. I turned in my pay record.

At this point, it must have been obvious that I was out of it because TFM said, "You clearly need a combat nap, wimp. I'll take you back, rack you and wake you up for chow." I stumbled into the hootch and collapsed into a sweaty, stinking heap of sleep on my rubber lady. It was the coolest thing I had felt all day. Temperature was near ninety-five degrees.

***

TFM woke me up at five. "Chow time," he said. "You'll get used to the heat after about two weeks," he told me, as we walked up the hill toward the mess hall. "Until then, it's like walking around under hot water." The only real temperature difference between the inside of the mess hall and the outside was that two big exhaust fans kept the air inside moving. The metal walls made the chow hall a sweatbox but at least the air was moving.

Mess hall food was good but mostly forgettable, although some aftereffects were not at all forgettable. We had just finished dessert, soupy half-melted ice cream, when those aftereffects hit me. I let TFM know something was screaming down my intestinal tract and wanted out. Now. He smiled and pushed back from the table. We bussed our steel trays and headed back down the hill, staying on the road. Gravity helped and hindered all at the same time. He pointed out the shitters and in I went, going through yet another screen door. He had advised me to look for some kind of toilet paper. I found a copy of *Stars and Stripes* newspaper and some C-rat-issue paper, just big enough to fold into a triangle and clean my fingernails with. But given the state I was in, that did not matter.

Six-hole outhouse at The Rose Garden. The only one-hole outhouse belonged to an only sometimes present but often maligned Task Force Delta general (*VMFA-115 1972–1973 Silver Eagles Cruise Book*).

At that moment on my very first day in The Rose Garden, I was introduced to the Nam Phong screamers. Any thought of privacy hit the plywood floor along with my utility trousers. I suppose I can be grateful that at least this first time the screamers hit me I was alone. Some kinds of misery don't love company. When the screamers were rampant in the Garden, all six seats were usually filled. Misery and company.

After the screamers ran their course, I squared away and walked bleakly back to the hootch. The rest of my other hootchmates were there, just back from afternoon hops, and TFM introduced me. I was still too preoccupied and fatigued to keep the three names and faces separate. There would be time for that later. I shucked off my boots, flopped down and passed out in a pool of sweat.

***

Near midnight, I was awakened to a groggy state by a cold wet feeling on my face. I opened my eyes and looked up to see the grinning mug of TFM. He proceeded to put one arm behind him, one arm across his chest and, using his knees, he began to move up and down like a fat piston, slowly at first, then built his rhythm and momentum to the point where I knew what was coming. He had a mouthful of beer and once his pumping reached climax speed, he spat the contents out of his mouth all over me. This was followed by maniacal laughter.

I had been given the fountain. I laughed and wiped myself dry. Then I listened to him berate me for all my shortcomings thus far as a Marine and RIO. Of course, he did all this in front of Weasel, Bush Hog, and Maggot, my other hootchmates. This was my unofficial welcome to the hootch and into the Silver Eagles. The other hootchmates joined in the berating some but not much. TFM knew me. They didn't, yet. They all did get a good laugh though. It was one of several rites of passage into an expeditionary Marine Corps. Into war.

***

Later I learned that the Squadron had already screened me before I had even arrived. My name was on a list of inbound orders that preceded me. All inbound men were screened at an All Officers Meeting, AOM. A canvass was taken of those who had known, or better, had flown with the incoming officer. The new guy's name would be brought forward and comments could be made openly. Some guys were blackballed and refused before they even arrived. Orders were changed if the right people talked to the right people. It was a survival issue for the Squadron. Over the next few days, I got to know my new hootchmates. All except TFM were former enlisted. All were pilots who had bootstrapped up to commissions through the Enlisted Commissioning Program, or ECP, a way up for stellar enlisted. They had worked hard to get their wings. TFM told me he had flown with all of them and they were good.

Looking back, this not-so-secret review-and-vote was a little mystifying, maybe scary, but it made sense. The opinion and judgment of a guy like TFM was in large part the basis on which we loaned our lives out for intense two-to-four-hour periods. In a war, by the time you find out firsthand someone isn't reliable, it may be too late. I learned the value of this process. We had to trust each other. Our words were good. They had to be. Often it was a matter of life or death.

***

The morning after that first night I woke up to a sound I did not expect and had never heard before. It was the sound of two empty five-gallon metal Jerry cans banging together, something like a metallic melancholic bass tone as the clanging and bumping went on. It was the original Maggot's turn to carry the Jerry cans down to the water buffalo, a wheeled tank where the potable water was kept. We took turns with this chore. The rule of hootch housekeeping was that if you were the one who emptied a Jerry can, you were the one who refilled it. Right then. We used the potable water for everything from drinking to shaving to making tea and coffee. Maggot had been shaving last and had emptied the cans. He was going to the water buffalo. We cold-water shaved outside the north end of the hootch under a canvas awning that was held up by tent poles. A piece of old perforated portable runway matting served as an all-weather outdoor deck. During heavy monsoon rains—there were no other kind, the ground where the hootches were at the bottom of the hill flowed with muddy water. For that reason, all the hootches were built two feet up off the red clay and sand.

Adjacent to the water buffalo was a five-foot-tall black rubber open-topped tank the size of a small outdoor swimming pool. Non-potable water. Once a week a tractor trailer tanker truck made a run to the local river, came back and filled up this tank. It was built with wooden slats

This five-foot-tall rubber tank held non-potable water for bathing and shaving. The water was trucked in from a local river and sometimes included dead critters. Best to keep your mouth closed! In this photograph, the author is cooling off in the water, an activity that felt good but was against the rules (*VMFA-115 1972–1973 Silver Eagles Cruise Book*).

molded internally to the reinforced rubber sides. It served well as long as it had water in it.

The usual bathing procedure was to walk down to the tank in flip-flops, naked as a jaybird, reach in, fill up a dishwashing bowl and pour the water over the naked body. Soap and shampoo optional. Repeat this process until clean. We called this procedure a *whore's bath*. The real trick was to finish before a six-by truckload of grunts came rolling down the road for a changing of the guard on the wire. The six-bys would coat a freshly cleaned guy with red dust. On top of that, infantry were known to jeer observations about an officer's anatomical equipment as they passed by. Loudly. Nothing to do about it. Just take it.

Once or twice dead critters were included in the truckload of river water dumped in the tank. They helped to enforce the unspoken rule of not swimming in the tank. We saw more than one dead dog floating there—another reason to keep your mouth closed tightly when bathing. If the unsanitariness of the indigenous Thai cook's helpers didn't give you the screamers first, a taste of the river water would.

***

The chow hall was a temporary structure, like everything else. Butane gas-bottle-fired burners served as field kitchens. Food was served in large industrial aluminum pans. Our food, like most Marine Corps food in those days, was good. The food was supposed to be *sufficient in quantity and quality*, as the standard logbook entry put it, but it wasn't the food that gave us the screamers. Our Thai mess men were not accustomed to personal cleanliness. They had not learned to wash their hands and their own toilet customs were primitive.

The food supply was under the charge of the Force Services Support Group, FSSG, stationed at Nam Phong. These men were professional Marines. Many of their officers were Mustangs, tough, older former enlisted who had earned commissions. Their collective best was very good.

But the Thai people who acted as kitchen helpers—country people who usually prepared their own food over smoldering charcoal fires—had a lot to learn not only about food preparation but also about hygiene. Rice with dead larvae in it was acceptable to them and we learned to shove the dead larvae to the side of the plate and keep eating. All of us ate as much as we could hold. The wisdom was to top off before a hop. We never knew when we would get to eat again.

The Marines who supervised the food preparation took their jobs personally. A huge African American master sergeant accosted me one day in the chow line because I passed up a pan of collard greens at his station. "Sir," he said, "I fixed those greens myself. You will hurt my feelings if you don't try some." No lieutenant in his right mind would knowingly offend a master sergeant, so I took some collards. At the table, I gingerly tried them with the best condiment ever made, Tabasco Sauce. I ended up going back for seconds and thirds. Each time, the Master Sergeant gave me a wide grin. They were the best collards I ever had, before or since. "See?" he said.

CHAPTER 4

Liberty

October 1972

During the Vietnam war, the term *liberty* wasn't used as a synonym for freedom except maybe in a minor personal way. It was official Marine and Navy language for time off granted at the discretion of a superior. *Leave* referred to a longer period of time charged against the 30 paid days per year Marines were allotted. Both *liberty* and *leave* were on our own nickel. By 1972, the days of government-sponsored rest-and-recreation-trips, R&R, were long gone. An indicator that the war was ending.

The rules for liberty, a program put in place long before I was around, were pretty straightforward. At The Rose Garden, there were two choices. An officer could take a two-day liberty to Udorn every two weeks or a three-day liberty to Bangkok once a month. I only went to Udorn except at the end of the war when we were in Bangkok as part of the retrograde, or pulling out. Liberty was restricted to these two places because of U.S. agreements with the Thai government. If we wanted to go elsewhere—like back home—we had to take leave, which required paperwork. It was a hassle. And costly, sometimes not just in money.

Like several guys I knew, I never took leave. Something inside me pushed back against extended time off during a war. It seemed wrong to be away, to be in a hotel. I wasn't gungey—a term derived from Gung Ho—or overly enthusiastic about the war. And my decision wasn't because I liked flying so much, which I did. It was really because leave could get expensive. I figured if I ended up *buying the farm*, getting killed, the least I could do was leave my wife with a decent amount of money. Plus I didn't feel right about returning to peacetime until war time, or my part of it, was done.

I re-thought that decision not to not take leave 13 years later during my first divorce. But at the time, I was distracted by some of the gut-ripping personal disaster stories that had happened to men on leave. More than one Marine officer returned to Nam Phong single after having gone on

33

leave married. I admit that I was worried about some of the risks that leave posed.

***

Udorn was in Thailand, about forty miles north of Nam Phong through the jungle. It was five miles from the Mekong River, which formed the border with Laos. In Udorn, Marines were restricted to the military installation and the town. Occasionally, someone would travel outside the town with permission but that was discouraged. Pathet Lao, Laotians who fought for the North Vietnamese Army, NVA, and the Viet Cong, were active in this area and they didn't take prisoners of war. They would kill us just to get the gold in our teeth or to keep from having to feed us or just for the hell of it. At least as a POW to the NVA or Viet Cong, we would have political currency. Could be a bargaining chip. The Laotians had no use for a prisoner and tribal politics were of the stone-age variety. So I had no desire to venture out of the U.S.-approved areas.

Assuming we had official business, officers could occasionally get to Udorn on one of The Rose Garden's two CH-46 helicopters. If we didn't have official business, we could try to snivel a hop on one of the copters. Lie, cheat and whine. But if we had hacked off one of the rotor heads, then we were out of luck for a chopper ride. The rotor heads at Nam Phong were a touchy, rank-conscious, non-combatant bunch. Gungey.

If we couldn't get a chopper ride, then we would be heading to Udorn on the Thai version of a rural bus, the infamous baht bus. At the time, Thai money, or baht, had a 20-to-1 exchange rate with the U.S. dollar. For a small amount of baht, we could pick up the bus right outside the wire and ride rough up to Udorn. Both officers and enlisted could ride the baht bus along with the rural Thai. We found ourselves journeying with their pigs, chickens, an occasional mutt dog and sometimes a monkey on a leash. It took our guys a bit of adjustment to be okay with the smells and behavior of the Thai, just as I am sure they had much to overcome about us.

Compared to what we had at The Rose Garden, Udorn AFB was the lap of luxury. Cement sidewalks, trimmed lawns, a real Officers Club, real beds and running water, which meant hot showers. We could also stay at the Charoen Hotel (pronounced *sharroan*). The CIA, which called itself Air America or just The Company, had a small headquarters there and had deemed the hotel safe. The Charoen's restaurant served delicious Thai food and some American dishes and had a pleasant ambiance. The place was well lit and had tables set with clean starched linens, spotless cutlery and beauti-

34

fully clear glassware. We could almost trick ourselves into thinking we were at a nice restaurant back in the world. But we weren't.

In the hotel's infamous Yellow Bird Bar, we often drank and visited with Air America guys. Although they would always evade or deny their connection, it was easy to pick them out. To begin with, they were Americans but with long hair. Trying to fit in, they wore Laotian drinking strings, gold trinkets and ID bracelets. They did some fine work as much as we knew, which was little.

The Yellow Bird Bar came complete with indigenous vocalists who had difficulty pronouncing the letter R which came out as an L. John Denver's "Country Roads" came out all wrong but the singer had his heart in the right place. The bar's theme song was "Butterfly," which was also the Thai-American colloquialism for a run-around lover. I heard more than one really angry Thai gal say to her Marine *du jour* on the street, "Why you buttafy me? You numbah ten!" She was calling him a bad man, the worst on the numerical scale. One day when I was in Udorn, I saw a woman chase a guy through the gate with a machete in her hand. The gate guards stopped her but the guy kept on running long after he crossed through the safety of the gates.

American money could buy most services or items we wanted or thought we needed. I leave the services to the imagination but I will say that a straight massage was a blessing and cheap. The Thai massages took place in a hotel on a floor designated for that alone. Each attendant wore a number on her smock and sat behind a glassed-in wall of a room. Because of the language barrier, and there was one, the customer selected the masseuse he wanted by asking for her number.

***

The first liberty I took after about a month at the Garden was a disconnected time. Being off was brand new to me and it felt like two days of stark nothing. I had a list of things to do. My hootchmates had given me a few suggestions. Of course, none of the things they suggested were things I really wanted or needed to buy. Except custom-fitted shoes and a shit-hot, our name for a one-piece party flight suit.

The Udorn shoe man, located near the taxi stand at the main gate, was unforgettable. He stood me on a clean sheet of drawing paper, traced both my feet, then took my money. For 14 American dollars, I could buy a custom-fitted pair of shoes or boots. I told him the color and style I wanted by pointing to a picture from a grimy catalogue. The next day my shoes were ready. I ordered two pairs of flying jodhpurs similar to a pair my Great-Uncle Creed had. The jodhpurs had wrap straps that circled the ankle and buckled. I got one pair brown and one black. The black pair was to be worn with my shit-hot. I took care of them, still have them, still wear them at special times like our one and only Silver Eagles reunion. Those shoes have held up so well that it wouldn't surprise me if they were made of water-buffalo hide. They still take and hold a shine. Like most Marines, I do know my shoe leather.

But the top item on my first Udorn shopping list was to get fitted for and buy a party suit. So I headed for the Maharajah Tailor—we corrupted the name of the place to Ram Jet's—just outside the main gate. As a serious civilian tailor, the Ram Jet's owner would custom-make and fit a regular suit or any kind of shirt we wanted but we used his expertise most often for our shit-hots. Every officer in Nam Phong had stashed his actual uniforms in Iwakuni, Japan, and would retrieve them on his way out. But we all needed a shit-hot.

The shit-hot was our unofficial formal wear, the dress uniform Commissioned Officers wore for the one fancy occasion in The Rose Garden, the Marine Corps Birthday, 10 November. The squadron also wore shit-hots to Happy Hours when a show of strength was mandated by the skipper, both at the Garden and during our one short-lived visit to Cubi Point in the Philippine Islands. I have no idea who started the shit-hot custom. Probably second- or third-tour men, veterans of Chu Lai or Da Nang.

The shit-hot was a civilian-style one-piece flight suit made in a squadron's colors. The squadron logo as well as the officer's individual callsign and rank were all patched or embroidered on. Our VMFA-115 shit-hots were blue with red, white and blue stripes shoulder to waist with an embroidered Silver Eagle just like the one on the rudder of our planes. We were young men then, had muscular butts and looked good in those shit-hots. I tried mine on many years ago. It didn't fit anymore.

***

The Maharajah Tailor Shop also made embroidered patches. Marines were allowed to wear only one patch on our uniform flight jackets—the squadron patch, the logo of the squadron we were currently assigned to. But each of us had a patch jacket in addition to the standard-issue cloth flight jacket. When a Marine's original cloth jacket wore out, it became his patch jacket. Sort of a rite of passage.

That patch jacket was more than just a make-do piece of clothing. It stated who we were by virtue of where we had been. Patches for all the other squadrons we had been in, our 100-mission patch, our 1,000-hour patch, all sewn onto the patch jacket. Patches were not the same as medals awarded even though they were both worn outwardly on occasions that called for them. Medals were part of the official uniform. Patches were part of the unofficial gear. Air Medals were formally awarded by Clipper after we earned a certain number of points. The requirement for an Air Medal was ten points, one point for each combat hop or two points if the plane took fire during the hop. The Forward Air Controller, FAC, over a bombing target was the one who had the say-so in that last matter.

An Air Medal was a big deal only to those who didn't have one yet. The Marines claimed they were equivalent to the Bronze Star. In reality, the Air Medal showed we had *been there*, along with the Vietnamese Campaign Medal and the Vietnamese Service Medal. An Air Medal was an official governmental award or decoration and therefore required a ceremony when it was presented. This award went in our Officers Qualification Record, OQR. In The Rose Garden, there was a slight departure from the normal Marine Corps hidebound approach for awarding the medal. The ceremony was held in a yet-to-be-occupied hootch where we held our AOMs. These were more than casual affairs. Our regular camp garb was jocks or skivvies or shorts with flip-flops but every Marine getting an Air Medal was required to wear a tee-shirt, color optional, so Clipper had somewhere besides our skin to pin the medal. I ended up with eight Air Medals. Several men I know had thirty or more.

The next medal up the chain was the Distinguished Flying Cross, DFC. In our squadron, we had a whopping total of two awarded to pilot and RIO for bringing back an airplane shot to pieces, including a hole in the wing that my flight jacket wouldn't be big enough to cover. The rumor was that in the O-Club in Udorn, the U.S. Air Force had a sign-up sheet, which read *To receive your end-of-tour DFC, sign here.* Some of our guys, so the rumor went, signed up. But they didn't get the DFCs.

Thirty-six years later, my second wife stealthily removed the patches from my patch jacket and had them mounted and framed. They are in my office, part of my I-love-me wall. They are a riot of color, although some bear dirt, grease and hydraulic fluid stains.

My kids have learned not to ask me what they mean. I tell them they are stickers from my personal suitcase.

CHAPTER 5

Housekeeping

October 1972–September 1973

A tour of a year included more than flying. Flying was, of course, the main thing, but when aircrew weren't flying, they had ground jobs, collateral duties. Part of being a Marine officer. We had known since we got our wings that we would always have two jobs. Lead men or train them to fight if you were a grunt, fly airplanes and do your ground job if you were an aviator. The Marine Corps did not abide idleness.

My first ground job after SLJO was as an assistant awards officer. Maddog was the other assistant to Kronor, our boss. We wrote everything: meritorious commendations from the skipper, air medal awards, nominations for the Distinguished Flying Cross. I got the job because I had been an English major in college.

For fun or to pass time until our hop briefs, we would write up fictitious award paragraphs and show them to each other. Maddog's were better than mine. They would start with verbiage like this: *Flat on his back at 40,000 feet, low on fuel, out of airspeed and out of ideas, clouds of lethal mosquitos on either wing, he dove straight down, guns ablaze, into a section of Vietnamese crop dusters, wiped them out and utterly destroyed three acres of enemy tomato plants at the same time with his afterburner plume.*

After our flight duties and past the normal hours for ground jobs, junior officers also knew that sooner or later, they had to stand the watch, a job known as squadron duty officer, SDO. It was an all-nighter job. The duty officer carried a sidearm and wore a cover to show his duty-authority. Theoretically, he was the direct representative of the squadron commander. That gave status to the temporary billet. In real life, we all knew if something big was going down, we would go wake up the XO, executive officer of the squadron. Let him tell the CO. The next morning, the XO signed-in the duty officer and read his carefully kept log before he turned the duty over to the relief man, another lieutenant. He would ask if there were any incidents or things that needed command attention. Usually, there weren't any or he would have known already. The log was mostly full of dry routine entries in military time, such as *0100. Toured the messing facilities for mid-rations. Food adequate in quantity and quality.* The night crew would have plenty to eat. A nightly tour of the squadron enlisted area was mandatory. The log entry usually said *0300. Tour of the squadron area made. All quiet.*

The group duty officer had a little more responsibility, sometimes more excitement. One night when another Marine was the group duty officer, a B-52 crash-landed at The Rose Garden.

If one was unlucky enough to have the duty, squadron or group, he might encounter rats that would sneak into the duty hootch, where stores of crackers, canned cheese and other goodies were stashed for the duty officers. I thought the rat business was idle talk until I had the group duty one night. I heard a scratching noise on the outside of the duty hootch screen and sure enough a Thai jungle rat, an honest foot-and-a-half long, was trying to get inside. That rat was smart and scooted down to the open end of the hootch, came right inside, trotted down the two-by-four and headed for the goody locker. I raised my .38 and nailed him with one shot aimed to climb over the hootch next door and not hit anyone. I made a logbook entry, *Spotted one rat, dispatched same.*

Another ground assignment for junior officers was paymaster for the unit. This job took a full day so the paymaster couldn't fly that day. Not a good thing. The job began at 5:30 a.m. at Disbursing, where pay in MPC, military payment currency, had to be counted out, received and signed for. The paymaster sat under an awning with his ammo cans of MPC. He wore a sidearm since pay was serious business. He had to hand-pay 200-odd people, who then had to count the pay back in front of him and sign as paid.

MPC was funny money. It was more colorful than U.S. currency but seemed not nearly as potent. The exchange rate of baht to U.S. dollars was at the time 20-to-1. That rate put a U.S. Marine corporal's pay in an enviable position. He could get a lot of baht for his MPC. Uncle Sam was aware of this currency value discrepancy and so used MPC instead of dollars for pay purposes. Said corporal was then at the mercy of the exchange sharks near Royal Thai Air Force Base Udorn, where most of us went for liberty, and had to negotiate the market. Officers intervened at times to keep our men from getting skinned. When payday ended, there had to be a signature for a certain amount of MPC per man and the books had to balance perfectly. Zero money at the end of the day or hell was raised. Small mistakes had to be tracked down and corrected immediately. Woe be unto the paymaster who ended up with five extra dollars MPC.

This job gave me a chance to put names with faces in the enlisted men's ranks and shoot the breeze about home, gifts to buy and other non-flying subjects. It was a chance not to think about 100 degree heat and 90 percent humidity for a while.

***

We also spent time on actual housekeeping as in *If you don't like the way your hootch is, fix it up.* Some guys took great pride in the appearance of their hootches, adding porches, awnings, and deck chairs, All home-made but functional. Some added wider-than-normal decks with purloined sheets of Marston matting. Some added rear porches for privacy. Ha Ha. Our troopers were more innovative in their home improvements than the officers. In fact, we held a contest with an award for the best spiffed-up hootch. The troopers got into it big time.

Appliances from home or the PX at Udorn frequently found their way to The Rose Garden. Almost every hootch had a tiny fridge in it. Ice cold water and tea were coveted. My friend Square had his parents send over a contraption used to heat his shaving water. The rest of us cold-water shaved. Regular electric fans were also prized items. In fact, a standard exchange between pilots and RIOs walking out to an airplane and the crew walking back in was *Hey, if you die, can I have your fan?*

Of course, anything electrically powered was at the mercy of the base's big diesel generators. An American man who was the representative of a U.S.-based contractor was stationed at the base. He had responsibility for the power supply and heard about it loudly at Happy Hour when the generators failed in the middle of the night, as they sporadically did. We got by as best we could. Jury rigging was the order of the day. As much as anything, dark-natured humor transformed into a funny joke helped as much as a decked-out hootch. After all, it was still a hootch with a rag top.

CHAPTER 6

Staying Human

October 1972

For Marines, the social highlight of the year is the Marine Corps Birthday Ball held annually on 10 November. A custom observed wherever in the world Marines are stationed, war or not, the Birthday Ball is a very big deal, probably celebrated in one way or another since 1776 when the Marine Corps was one year old. One year older than the United States of America. Stateside, the Ball is an elaborate affair, complete with a Marine Corps–wide protocol closely followed. At Birthday Balls, the youngest and oldest Marines in attendance are recognized and a decorated cake is ceremoniously escorted in. Then the oldest Marine cuts the cake with a ceremonial sword and serves the youngest.

Someone reads the letter from Gen. John A. LeJeune, storied Commandant of the Marine Corps, making the Birthday Ball more or less official policy. Toasts are raised to the President of the United States, the Commandant of the Marine Corps and usually to the Queen of England. Many Marine customs were borrowed from the British Royal Marine Corps. It is always a good time. We have a good meal and informal custom says it is the only time Marines are unofficially allowed to drink as much as they can hold and then some.

In my post–Vietnam life, I attended some memorable Marine Corps Birthday Balls. During my command of 96th ANGLICO in Florida, entertainment at the Birthday Ball was the entry of a troop of bagpipers and four riflemen carrying flintlock rifles. The fanciest Birthday Ball I ever attended was held by VMFA-112 in Dallas. Service members wore the Marine evening mess dress—navy blue pants with a red stripe and a black jacket—or the Class A uniforms. Medals, ribbons and badges are *de rigueur*. Women guests wore ballgowns.

But the Birthday Ball held on 10 November 1972, in The Rose Garden was like none I had been to before and none I have been to since. Officers wore their shit-hots. Troopers could attend in the uniform of the day. There were no wives or sweethearts since ours were absent so someone brought a blow-up doll complete with smeared lipstick. We all took turns dancing with her and she followed well. The meal and the cake were good. The drinking strong.

It was difficult to follow custom and ceremony in the Thai jungle but we did what we could. And way beyond custom and ceremony, we improvised on many of the typical activities men do for fun, including sports, various kinds of entertainment and Happy Hours. And we created some new ways to humanize ourselves too. We played jungle-rules volleyball games almost daily after a visit to the chow hall. Somehow a set of posts with a steel cable across the top had been installed in our company street. Pilots would play against RIOs or maybe hootch would play against hootch, borrowing a player or two when necessary.

One night, the Silver Eagles even had a match against the Red Devils from 232. It was a rough match. The steel cable across the top of the posts prevented much reaching over to interfere but we tried. Two of my hootchmates, Maggot and Bush Hog, were on opposing sides. Maggot, the taller man, went up against Bush Hog, reaching over the cable to block the shot. That put him high off the ground and as he came back down, he landed sideways on his ankle and was writhing in the dirt, obviously in pain. Bush Hog went up to him and said, "Shit hot! Now I can get your hops!" Getting combat hops was highest priority among a bunch of competitive fighter pilots and RIOs but Maggot recovered without incident and didn't lose a single hop.

***

In the fall, despite the 95 degree weather and 95 percent humidity, we decided we should have a flag football tournament. We played our games on a hard red-clay field. Even though 232 had a former pro player from the Dallas Cowboys on their team, the Silver Eagles won the championship. I was the center and Beak, who had been a standout high school quarterback, played anywhere we needed him. The usual rule that forbade officers from fraternizing with enlisted men was suspended. Several enlisted saw a chance to knock an officer on his can and they did.

***

Once or twice a week, we had a movie. In a common area near officers' country, two four-by-eight-foot pieces of painted-white plywood were stood side-by-side and attached to standing poles. By December, we had showers one night a week and a wag would come into the shower and announce the movie for the night as a running joke. I remember the fake announcement of *The Guns of Navarrone, Gidget Goes Hawaiian,* and *The Magnificent Seven.* What we might actually see, though, would turn out to be something like *The Living Desert* or *It's a Wonderful Life.* Everyone went to the movie anyway—VMA-533, the A-6 guys, 115, 232, MABS and HAMS, the Headquarters and Maintenance Squadron. The grunts were invited but they never came. The remarks from the peanut gallery were often more entertaining than the films, especially if a gecko lizard ran across the plywood screen. But that was better than nothing. When there was nothing, we stayed in the hootches, coming up with Monopoly games, Scrabble games, card games. Maybe we used the time to write letters or make tapes to send home. Or we just harassed each other.

We would go to the O-Club, which we called the Tiki Hut, if there was a local singer or other entertainment but that was rare. On Friday night at the club, we had Happy Hour. The units rotated Happy Hour sponsorship, providing snacks and making sure we had adequate liquor. To get the liquor, the squadron SLJO would be given time to go up to Udorn on a baht bus or, if he was lucky, he could snivel a hop on one of two CH-46 helicopters attached to Task Force Delta and make a quick trip of it. When I had this job as SLJO, I got to Udorn on a chopper and paid Thai helpers to work with me to load the liquor on another chopper for the flight back. Mission accomplished.

Some Happy Hours provided a time for squadrons, dressed in their best shit-hot party suits, to show off their unity and bravado through singing dirty songs or by hiring bands of local Thai singers who would come and do their best. One Friday night, the hosts were our grunts from 3/9 attached to Task Force Delta as security forces. Everyone was looking around for snacks when the grunt officers rolled in a wheelbarrow full of C-rations. That went over like a lead balloon and we made fun of those grunts and booed them loudly.

***

On sunny days, it was not uncommon to see five or ten men lying naked on cots behind the hootches *baking their snakes.* Our flight docs had given us a little message that the male member was particularly vulnerable to sunburn but one or two guys fell asleep sunbathing face up and lived with the painful consequences. The only time I remember that we were told to knock off the nudity was when the one-and-only Bob Hope show came to The Rose

Garden to entertain us. Since there were women in Hope's entourage, we were told to remain fully clothed all day for the three days of the visit.

***

Some strange shenanigans but they helped us remain human in spite of everything else.

CHAPTER 7

Task Force Delta?

October 1972

When I arrived at RTAFB Nam Phong, I had never heard of Task Force Delta, TFD. Maybe my orders mentioned it but all I saw when I looked at those orders was Nam Phong. I didn't even know TFD was an entity until I saw a shoulder patch on some guy's flight jacket that said *Task Force Delta, 90–120 days.* Later I saw this patch as a pointed joke. Task Force Delta had been at Nam Phong since April 1972. By September when I got there, it had overstayed its welcome by 90 days. TFD did not, in fact, cease until August 1973, one year and one month after the 120-day limit it set for itself at the outset.

Admittedly, I was very green when it came to command structures in the Marine Corps. I was a first lieutenant who had been in only one line squadron. I knew I was a member of a Wing that had a two-star general in charge, a Marine Air Group that had a bird colonel in charge, and a squadron that had a lieutenant colonel in charge. In September 1972, I'd never heard of a Marine task force with a general in charge but by September 1973, that would change. I learned that Task Force Delta was an actual command, headed up by a one-star general, who was in The Rose Garden, off and on, then out doing *general things.*

The assets subordinate to the TFD General, besides two F-4 squadrons and one A-6 squadron, included a Force Service Support Group, FSSG, responsible for roads, food, etc.; two KC-130 tankers; two CH-46 helicopters; a fuel distribution system; and an airport maintenance outfit, which included a huge cherry picker that could lift an F-4 out of the mud. TFD also owned crash crew and manned the airport control tower. These assets were not organic to a Marine Air Group but they were necessary for the overall operation of The Rose Garden.

The Task Force Delta staff, thin on people, served as liaison staff to the disparate elements attached to it. As far as I know, they were all noncombatants. Some Naval aviators were on the staff but they did not fly with the line units of MAG-15. They were overworked and frustrated, probably wanted to be doing what we were doing—flying in combat.

The most senior permanent man at The Rose Garden was the MAG-15 commanding officer, a colonel whose callsign was Joker. On paper, TFD was the senior command but the true authority for day-to-day operations rested with Joker and where and when the rubber really met the road, the squadron commanders were the on-scene tactical bosses. Including my CO Clipper. That made things hazy.

The junior officers resented TFD's presence because they appeared to be superfluous and often ineffective. We needed things they were supposed to get for us, such as a PX where we could get haircuts, consistent medical care, beds, nets, road tar, pipe and jeeps. We rarely got those things. With the exception of bombs and jet fuel, we went mostly without, sometimes had the barest of minimums and had to adapt. At the very end of my tour, I ate C-rations for two weeks. More than many grunts in the jungle had, but hardly the food *sufficient in quality and quantity* that all of us were supposed to have.

More to the point, we did the flying. They shuffled paper. Just another bureaucratic pain in the ass. Unlike us, they did not have any literal skin in the game. What I saw of Task Force Delta as a young first lieutenant was colored by this organizational tension and these conflicting roles. Several events during my tour, some humorous, some serious, relate to this uneasy relationship.

***

We mainly paid little attention to Task Force Delta until its general showed up on base. Then we begrudgingly paid due respect. I met the TFD general after a snafu on my first hop. Nothing personally came of that but I knew who he was. During that meeting, I picked up Clipper's careful but clear nonverbal communication that this TFD and its general were something to be put up with. Nothing he could do.

The TFD general, the only one around at the time, felt he was due privileges of rank. One of those privileges was sleeping in an air-conditioned trailer all to himself. The only other souls that got that perk were Bob Hope and his cast when they came to give us the USO show. People understood air-conditioning for Bob Hope. They did not understand a Marine general sleeping in air-conditioning while everybody else sweated it out. But what could anyone do?

Chapter 7. Task Force Delta?

Aha. Another perk the general required was his own private one-hole outhouse, his very own shitter. Some of the TFD staff painted it red and emblazoned it with a big white single star, lest anyone doubt who the owner might be. The outhouse was situated near the TFD headquarters hootches. The troopers at the Garden couldn't pass that up. Late one night, with the general back in Iwakuni, some troopers clandestinely put a rope around the red shitter, toppled it over and hauled it away. The toppling made the rounds on the jungle grapevine and all the junior officers and troopers had a good laugh.

The TFD staff hit the roof and immediately took the general's outhouse back to its proper location and re-installed it. And no sooner was it re-installed than it was moved away again. And again. We kept on laughing. Finally, Group S-4 Logistics was ordered to secure the outhouse. Whatever it took. What it took was several engineer stakes and many feet of light cable. When they finished, the shitter looked like a steel-wrapped cocoon.

During the time these shenanigans were going on, the general decided to make a personal call on Clipper at his hootch. Some of Clipper's men were invited over to chat with the general. Clipper had known him from times past and had told us he was really a pretty good guy. And a good shot in the F-8, a retired fighter that carried an internal gun/cannon. OK. So we sat through a hand of Liar's Poker or two and humored our skipper and made nice with the general. Clipper cleaned his clock in the poker match and the general called it a night.

***

One night at a fairly liquor-soaked Happy Hour, the TFD chief of staff, a lieutenant colonel, callsign Moose, got some ribbing from my later boss, callsign Rat. Or it could have been vice versa. Maybe it was about being a staff weenie and not flying combat. Maybe they were just playing cards and the trigger was a point of honor in the card game. Whatever it was, the underlying tension in the organizational relationship bubbled up. I was nearby with other junior officers and heard what was going on. In seconds, Rat and Moose were face to face, close and angry. Cursing in raised voices. As it turned out, the almost-tussle came to nothing. The two men backed off but they did not make peace. I saw once again that frustrations were very high between TFD and our guys.

***

Section One—My New World

With the clarity of hindsight and the passage of time, I understand now that the work of Task Force Delta headquarters was a thankless job. Men had been sent to a hole in the jungle with few assets and inadequate personnel to keep a taskforce with its scope of work functioning and effective.

Section Two

Hops

CHAPTER 8

The Phantom, in Brief

A civilian friend once warned me that part of my Rose Garden story sounded like an owner's manual for the F-4 Phantom. But we were Marine fighter pilots and RIOs, and the heart of what we did during our time in the Garden—flying combat hops—will not really make sense without some brief overview of the bird we flew.

With two big strong engines, GE J79-8s, the Phantom could exceed twice the speed of sound if it was well maintained and clean, not carrying any external loads. I know it could because I did it and I have the pin from McDonnell-Douglas to prove it. The plane had an on-board manually operated analog navigation computer. I didn't learn how to operate that computer and spin the knobs used to update it until I was in theater. Spinning those knobs was a trick while pulling up off a bomb run with five to six Gs on the bird, sometimes upside down.

The Phantom was built around two missiles systems, a long-range Sparrow that required a radar jock to guide it, and a Sidewinder or heat-seeker. The Phantom could carry in bomb tonnage close to the same amount that a B-17 carried in World War II. It also had nuclear capability and could carry a 20-millimeter gun pod and an array of ballistic rockets up to five-inches in diameter. The Phantom could refuel in flight with its retractable pop-out refueling probe that stayed locked behind a hydraulically operated door until it was needed. The retractable refueling probe was a supersonic speed consideration. The Phantom guzzled gas. Later models had fuel gauges in the back seat but in the earlier ones the RIO had to ask the pilot for the fuel remaining and keep his mind on it.

Just about anything the plane could do—fighting air-to-air or bombing air-to-ground—took the collaboration of the two-man crew that flew it, a pilot in the front seat and a RIO in the back. The front and back seats were covered by separately operating clear Lexan canopies. RIOs always ran the radar. There were no radar controls in the front cockpit, only repeater scopes. And RIOs served as a second set of eyes to identify bogeys, or

A fully loaded F-4 with canopies open taxiing out for a hop. The canopies were closed shortly before takeoff. Each plane carried the following information: VE, squadron designator; VMFA-115, squadron number; 153062 (partially hidden), Bureau of Naval Aviation number; 3 (out of 14 planes in the squadron), side number. A silhouette of a Silver Eagle, the squadron logo, is on the plane's rudder (*VMFA-115 1972–1973 Silver Eagles Cruise Book*).

bad guys. RIOs usually ran the radios but some pilots who didn't grow up with the F-4 did their own talking. Most of them were old hard-headed single-seaters when they were younger. RIOs laughed at their screw-ups. Navigation duties also usually fell to RIOs but pilots often chimed in to correct things. I'm glad they did. Both our rear-ends were in the plane. The long and short of it was that our lives were in their hands and theirs in ours.

In a worst-case scenario, if our pooch was truly screwed and pilot and RIO had previously agreed on the decision, from the back seat the RIO could initiate ejection of both crew. In combat, I never had to punch out myself or eject my pilot, even though I did come close. Truth be told, RIOs generally tried to ride herd on the pilots. We even sang at times to calm them down.

I'm pretty sure that every person who flew that plane thought it was the most fighter-looking jet ever built. The Phantom could take a licking and keep on ticking. It looked predatory and fearsome, even parked on a flight line. And it was gorgeous to boot.

CHAPTER 9

First Hop

October 1972

First combat hop. 27 October 1972, a few weeks after my arrival in Nam Phong. Like all combat hops, this one involved a Section, or two airplanes—one plane, the Lead; the other, the Wingman, called Dash-two or just Two. My first hop was a hootch hop, which meant that guys from my own hootch would be on it. Maggot was the Lead pilot with Fat Maggot as his RIO. Bush Hog was my pilot in the Wingman plane. Bush Hog was a demanding, often edgy, sometimes abrasive pilot but TFM said he was good. I knew I had best have my shit together.

I was as nervous as one could get and still be able to function. The 270.8 hours of flying time I had under my belt were feeling pretty thin. I knew my way around the plane and I really liked to fly but going into possible fire on my first combat hop was different. I worried about how I would do. Would I nerve-puke or shit myself? Would I—could I—hack it? But mostly, I wondered if I would show fear? Could I build a reputation of trust and reliability? Would pilots want to go into combat with me as their RIO?

Flight briefs in Vietnam took longer than they did in the States, about an hour and a half total. We got sporadic intelligence reports on what to expect and roughly where we were going. On this hop, it was the *Plaine des Jarres*, Laos, the PDJ, a true valley plain ringed in by high jungle mountains. The jars the place was named for were large burial urns favored by the old Laotian culture. Several roads and trails out of North Vietnam intersected there and both motorized and foot traffic moved through night and day. All combat air in Nam Phong had been working this area for a while. The area was heavily defended in places. A surface-to-air missile (SAM) ring was not too far away. SAMs came in a range of sizes with the biggest, the SAM-2, the size of a telephone pole. The smallest was the shoulder-mounted SAM-7. We all knew SAM rings were truck-mounted and could be sent to reinforce an area if it was important enough. The PDJ at that time was important enough.

Section Two—Hops

We were mainly after large fixed-weapons emplacements, supply dumps, lines of communication or trucks carrying people and supplies. But our targets could and did change rapidly, depending on the situation on the ground. We would go after whatever we were told to. We would be assigned to work a general area for weeks at a time and then suddenly be shifted somewhere else. We never knew until we checked in with airborne command and control, ACC, after aerial refueling, and got the scoop. We did not have the big picture. We had the little picture, which was starkly clear.

On this particular day, as Bush Hog and I walked around for inspection of our Phantom before the hop, he showed me what to pay particular attention to—safety pins, fuses, pigtails or electrical plugs, bombs and lugs, cannon plugs, rockets, external fuel tanks and leaks—white ones were gas; red, hydraulic fluid; brown, oil. No leaks anywhere. We also checked the missiles. The load this day was the heaviest I had seen carried routinely on the airplane—ten 500-pound bombs, called Mark 82s; four five-inch Zuni rockets for flak suppression; one AIM-9 Sidewinder missile; one AIM-7 Sparrow missile; and two 370-gallon external fuel tanks.

The mission was to drop bombs in close or direct air support but if we were jumped by enemy MiGs, we could shoot them in the face with the Sparrow or shoot them in the tailpipe with the Sidewinder. The extra 4,500 pounds of gas in the externals was often the difference between a silk descent in a parachute and a Phantom's normal landing at home plate. The planes were also heavy because they carried working radar homing and warning gear. The RHAW gear told us if the bad-guy radar was looking at us. We seldom carried RHAW gear when we trained in the States because all working gear had been sent to Wes-Pac, Navy shorthand for Western Pacific. Vietnam. Wes-Pac was the priority.

The RHAW gear would either light up or sound off in our helmets or both if our plane was in the enemy's radar beams. Each situation called for a different set of responses. We could jink—evade violently—or shoot flares to confuse some of the heat-seeking SAMs. We could also blow chaff out the side of the plane to confuse inquisitive radars. Chaff was made up of aluminum strips cut to half the wavelength of the enemy's radar. A cloud of these strips made a blot on the enemy's radar scope, a cloud that could cause confusion, maybe resulting in a near miss, which was surely better than a direct hit.

Bush Hog had been good about telling me what I really needed to know. We were ready. My first combat hop, not a training hop. Big difference. Real bullets, maybe a SAM. We boarded up and strapped in, started the engines,

Chapter 9. First Hop

Five of this F-4's load of ten Mark-82 500-pound bombs, highly and capriciously decorated as Easter eggs around Easter time 1973, are being loaded by an enlisted ground supervisor or plane captain (*VMFA-115 1972–1973 Silver Eagles Cruise Book*).

radio checked, taxied and stopped at the end of the runway for arming. Ground crewmen came to pull out the safety pins that prevented bombs and missiles from detonating on the ground, wrap them in their red flags and then show them to me. Then they stowed the pin bundle in the back of the plane inside a small door called the hell-hole for re-use on another hop.

The Lead plane had already taken position on the runway. The canopies closed. We taxied out, stopped briefly and were cleared for takeoff. The standard hop routine was for the two planes, Lead and Two, to join up airborne as soon as possible after takeoff to double-check each other for potential problems. We checked by flying close aboard—wing-tip-to-wing-tip in a 36-inch stepdown. Then we crossed underneath each other, looking for leaks, spinning fuses or prematurely armed bombs and we counted bombs and missiles.

Our takeoff and climb-out were uneventful. We joined up behind and below Lead to check his bombs. Maggot was clear so we crossed under him, gave him a thumbs-up and stayed steady. He dropped down, crossed under us and popped out on the other side. Everything seemed to be going well until TFM asked me, "Two, how many bombs did you take off with?" "Ten," I answered.

I will never forget TFM's next comment, "Well, you only have nine now." I was ready for some scary shit to be given to me on my first hop but I knew TFM well enough to know when he wasn't bullshitting. He was quietly serious. Bush Hog and I went over the situation. We had felt nothing strange during takeoff. We saw no detonation on the ground and had no indication that anything was amiss. We talked it over with the Lead plane. Maggot was okay with continuing on so we did. My internal tension meter twisted up a notch because I knew no one was kidding around now. About anything. All of this was real.

We headed north with the Mekong River coming up on the nose. Then we were across the fence. We switched on our RHAW gear and I opened the bucket doors to test-fire a chaff bundle and one flare. Standard procedure called for us to pop one of each just to make sure they worked—left side, right side. TFM switched frequencies and we came up on the command-and-control frequency. We checked in and were given the call-sign and vector that would get us to our on-scene commander, the forward air controller. We found the FAC with our eyeballs and TFM gave him our line-up—who we were, how much time on station—time we could give, and what kind of ordnance we carried. He responded with the target description, type of defensive fire to expect, the best bail-out in case we were hit and, most importantly, the target elevation and altimeter settings. We had to reset the barometric reading on the altimeter to tell us our altitude for that particular area. No one wanted to fly into the ground. That could ruin the whole day.

Our FAC then told us when and how he would mark the target and said he would adjust our runs verbally from Lead's mark, where he dropped his bombs. The FAC marked the target with a smoke rocket, which we called a *willie pete* for its white phosphorus, and then gave adjustments on the smoke. Maggot and TFM were about a half-mile from us, 180 degrees out in heading on the race-track pattern we flew while we waited to acquire the target. The Lead plane was already cleared hot, or ready to bomb, and down they went. When Maggot was ready, he released his first five bombs and pulled up to a safe altitude to re-enter the race-track pattern. It was grim and magnificent to watch Maggot's bombs do their work. They created billows of fire, smoke and earth. They were audible as mild whumps.

The FAC said, "Two, twelve o'clock on Lead's hits, one click. Cleared hot." He told us to go one kilometer north of the Lead plane's hits. We were cleared to bomb. We rogered and called, "Two's in hot."

Bush Hog pointed the nose up, rolled the F-4 on its back and pulled down to a 30-degree dive angle on our run-in line, then flipped the plane upright and lit the burners. I was totally focused on the run trying to sequence the calls I had to make. As the altimeter unwound rapidly and the airspeed built, I got a singer-low tone in my headset, much like a slow version of the sirens European police cars use. An Eee Oooh sound. Somebody was looking at us but I stayed riveted to the gauges. I asked Bush Hog if he had anything. He said nothing and I kept the calls coming despite the RHAW gear's noise.

I pumped out a bundle of chaff for insurance while feeling sweat flush out of my body. We had one more run to make and I wasn't going to make it easy on the SAMs. I knew Bush Hog had heard the tones from the RHAW gear but he kept right on flying at the proper speed and dive and angle. He did not jink to evade any threat. I called, "Stand by, stand by. Mark!" at the right time and felt the shotgun charges blow the bombs off our plane as Bush Hog began to pull up. I felt the G-force come on the Phantom as we climbed up and re-entered the race-track pattern. Right then I was little more than baggage but I did remember to twist around and see where the bombs hit. Later, I learned to look for secondary explosions after the bombs went off. The secondaries would tell us if war materiel in the targets had been hit.

The music of the RHAW gear sounded off again. My heart was pumping hard until I heard Bush Hog say quietly but with some aggravation, "All right, you two. Knock it off." Then he said to me, "Fat Maggot's just messing with you. There are no SAM rings up here. You swallowed it. Part of the Fucking New Guy drill." We circled high and dry, all *switches safe*, and joined up for the lookover.

Both planes had done two runs each and we awaited our bomb damage assessment, BDA, which only the FAC could give. We received it and were cleared to switch frequencies for return to base. We flew close aboard again, checking each other for visible gun hits and hung bombs, unexpended ordnance, leaks. All clean. We were formation flying close to each other and I looked over at TFM. He had his oxygen mask off, was laughing and making obscene gestures. I gave him one back and we headed home. He had hit the test button on the RHAW gear and broadcast it to me through the voice mic in his mask. I bit on it, being an FNG. The rest of the flight was uneventful. That is more than I can say about our reception after landing.

***

Section Two—Hops

Our Task Force Delta General was waiting to greet us. A one-star who remains nameless in my memory. With him was our Group CO, a full colonel; Clipper, a lieutenant colonel; our Safety Officer; and the Chief of Staff of Task Force Delta, another lieutenant colonel.

The General went straight up to Bush Hog while our skipper watched, shrugging his shoulders at us as if it were some kind of signal. The TFD General asked Bush Hog, "Didn't you know you dropped a bomb on the runway when you took off, son?" and he looked over at me with no change of expression.

"No, sir, we didn't. Not until we were pretty far north of the field. There were no problems so we pressed," said Bush Hog, rationalizing why we had kept on with the hop.

"Do you know what became of your bomb?" the General asked, looking straight into my eyes.

"No, sir, we don't," I responded, using the plural pronoun because whatever happened to the RIO happened to the pilot too, and vice versa. The crew concept.

"There it goddamn is!" The General pointed to the north end of the runway to an EOD truck, the explosive ordnance disposal vehicle used in bomb defusing. "It fell off, slid down the runway, armed itself, and landed fuse up in the berm! Don't you ever fucking do that again! If you shit a bomb, you RTB!" he shouted at us as a spray of spittle left his lips. He meant it. We should have returned to base. A meek "Aye, aye, sir," came from Bush Hog and me.

The General turned to his lieutenant colonel and said, "Let's go see those monkeys in the tower. They musta been asleep. Shoulda seen that bomb when it came off. Goddammit!" Our skipper was listening to his skipper but had given us the no-big-deal wave-off.

***

I didn't spend too much time thinking about what would have happened if the fallen bomb had detonated under our fully loaded F-4 as we took off. It was pointless to think about. The bottom line was it didn't. Later that night, we heard a muffled whump when the bomb was detonated out in the safe-blast area. We were deep into the tequila and beer by then. I had been toasted for surviving my first hop.

***

I learned it wasn't unusual for things to go awry on a first hop. Bush Hog's brother Fox was a pilot with our sister squadron in Nam Phong,

Chapter 9. First Hop

VMFA-232. We called them *the girls next door*, which is also what they called us. On Fox's first hop, a 57-millimeter-gun round hit his bird perpendicular to the fuselage and shot away the parachute horseshoe at the top of his ejection seat. The horseshoe would activate the escape system that got the main escape chute open. After losing his horseshoe, Bush Hog's brother could not have punched out if he had needed to.

My own first hop seemed less significant after hearing that tale.

***

I flew twice a day for the next two days, got a day off, then had two more days of two-a-day, all red ink. In the logbook, actual combat hops were recorded in red ink. Training hops, or, as we called them, day-fuck-arounds, were recorded in black ink. They were mostly post-maintenance check flights.

I was no longer the FNG. Ten combat hops in my first week of flying. I was glad for the intensity. I was over the shakes, thought I knew what to expect and was focused on becoming better at what we were doing. I knew now that I could do it but at the time, I didn't realize that I would end up liking it enough to try to become exceptional at it. I never did become really exceptional. But I damned sure tried to.

CHAPTER 10

Bringing Back the Hose

November 1972

I truly believe that the Creator keeps life interesting for those who pay attention so I'm never surprised when the Creator throws me a high, hot, hanging curve ball.

One of the curveballs in my life was Handsome, a nickname that my friend gave himself, of course, and that eventually stuck as his callsign. He had the energy of a tsunami. You didn't meet Handsome. He met you. And when he did, he introduced himself as Handsome. He might physically pick you up and throw you down or at least crush your hand in a vise-like grip. He had the vitality and joy of living of at least three people and the strength of two, maybe more. All in one body with the physique of a gorilla. He had been a collegiate wrestler and football player, a linebacker. He was one of several guys I flew with who forced the airplane into what he wanted it to do. Forget finesse. Handsome's stick moves were main strength.

He would fly anything, anytime, anywhere, under any circumstance. He didn't care if he was flying a test hop, a combat hop, a weather recon, or if he was just boring holes in the sky. What Handsome cared about was getting airborne. Then he was his best self.

Handsome had more fighter pilot aggression than almost anyone else I ever saw. That aggression cost me personally on a test hop back in North Carolina, where he and I were in VMFA-312 together. We took the bird up and out over the Atlantic Ocean off Cherry Point to check it out after lengthy official rework. We needed to test all the systems that had supposedly been repaired. The airplane worked fine and we had gas left to burn, which translated into free flight time. He wanted to head up toward Naval Air Station, NAS, Oceana, near Norfolk, Virginia, to shoot some touch and go's, or do landing practice, and then return to Cherry Point. That sounded okay to me since we were already halfway there. We swung northwest and I switched the radio frequency to approach control for Oceana. All routine.

I had my head down working the radar to see if anyone was in front

Chapter 10. Bringing Back the Hose

of us. I started to look outside and the instant I did, my head was slammed back down into the radar screen. If I hadn't had my helmet on and visor down, I would have broken my nose. Handsome had put an instantaneous eight-G, low-slice left turn on the plane and lit the afterburners all at the same time. I could not lift my head up and believe me, I tried. Under normal circumstances I was a pencil neck with a four-pound head and two-pound helmet. I could feel my neck muscles strain and pop as I tried to lift what had suddenly become a 32-pound head and 16-pound helmet.

Handsome had spotted two Navy F-8 single-seat fighters below us, flying along fat, dumb and happy. They were breaking the unwritten rule among fighters—*always check your six*. Make sure no one *ever* gets behind you for a shot. If a plane was flying along fat, dumb and happy and was *not* keeping a lookout, as that F-8 was not, the plane was fair game and could expect to be jumped or attacked from the blind spot. Handsome had jumped the F-8s without telling me he was going to dive and turn. He had excellent eyesight and perfect reflexes and was doing what he had been trained to do. Be aggressive. But it took two weeks for me to get over the sprained neck.

***

Right before most of us were shipped overseas, we had had one last squadron party at Cherry Point. The party house was at the end of a long gravel road that sat beside Albemarle Sound. Everyone had arrived that night except Handsome and a group had gathered out on the porch in the dark, speculating as to where he was. Then someone spotted headlights close together, approaching the house. "There he comes in the fighter jeep," someone said. "Has to be him."

As we all watched, the jeep tried to take a tight curve. We could see the headlights scribe a tall vertical circle, stop and then return to where they began with a bounce. Dust was everywhere. "He rolled it," someone yelled. Handsome roared up in a cloud of dirt and gravel and jumped out of the rolled jeep, grinning. Another voice called out, "Handsome, your arm is cut!" He looked down and said, "Yeah, I over-G'd that turn but made a decent recovery." He started to laugh. One of the wives took him inside, washed the blood off his arm and patched it up. He stayed the length of the party. No big deal.

***

When an F-4 based in The Rose Garden rendezvoused with a KC-130 tanker to refuel in the air, the fighter plugged its retractable probe into the tanker's refueling apparatus, which was held in two baskets attached to 85-foot steel and rubber hoses that came out on either side of the tanker. The baskets gave the tanker its callsign Basketball. The receptacles mated with the F-4's refueling probe and gave gas, everything happening while the plane was going 230 knots. This process required a certain precision and was not without its perils. In an attempt to disconnect or back the probe out from the tanker, the refueling apparatus could malfunction and the Phantom would be locked to the KC-130 by the 85-feet of hose.

If this happened, the tanker had a switch that would guillotine the hose, leaving about 50 feet of steel and rubber attached to the extended probe of the Phantom. If the hose and basket didn't blow off, they would whip back into the airstream parallel to the fuselage and begin beating the Phantom to pieces. Not a good scenario. This exact situation happened to Handsome. The hose badly beat up the airplane but broke neither canopy. Bits of the wing were mashed and small chunks of the wing's trailing edge were missing but Handsome managed to fly back to the Garden and land without further incident. His flying skills and exact compliance with emergency procedures saved the crew and the plane.

A KC-130 tanker with baskets streaming on 85-foot rubber hoses, as seen from an F-4, 200 feet below and aft. Two F-4s could refuel simultaneously from each tanker (*VMFA-115 1972–1973 Silver Eagles Cruise Book*).

Chapter 10. Bringing Back the Hose

This photograph was taken by the author from the back seat of his Phantom in the Lead position. The Wingman or Two plane in his Section of planes is about to plug-in and refuel from the KC-130 tanker (author's collection).

Our *VMFA-115 1972–1973 Silver Eagles Cruise Book*—sort of like a high school yearbook—has a picture of the bird on the ramp with the basket still stuck on it. And one of the stainless-steel grommets from the very basket that Handsome brought back adorns my desk. It is twisted 90 degrees out of its original shape and broken in half. If I am having a less than stellar day, I take a moment to look at the grommet. The man could fly.

***

One day I was walking back to my hootch in The Rose Garden. Handsome came up to me with a concerned look on his face. Unusual for him. His father, a Marine Hellcat pilot in World War II, had died back in the world. Handsome was tasked with the job of taking his dad's ashes up to about 15,000 feet and scattering them out an open window in the plane.

He was from a well-off family but he asked me if I had 25 bucks in cash that he could borrow to make the trip back to the States. I said sure. Money was not something any of us ever worried about with each other. Weeks later when he returned, he unselfconsciously wrote me a check in the most artistic handwriting I had ever seen. But then he did everything with flair. Handsome was one of those people who could drive even the most patient

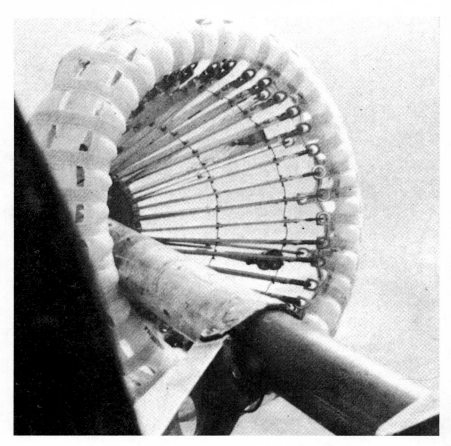

Close-up of an F-4 receiving fuel while plugged into the tanker basket, as photographed from the back seat of a Phantom in the Lead plane of the Section (*VMFA-115 1972–1973 Silver Eagles Cruise Book*).

person insane. Unless you were in his back seat, that is. I know few who were better pilots and I never watched or worried about anything he did airborne, war or peace. But I knew from personal experience always to brace for hard turns when I was working or playing with Handsome.

CHAPTER 11

Silence from the Backseat

November 1972

Maggot came to Nam Phong as a captain from a West Coast Marine F-4 squadron where he went by the callsign Dirtman. He was rechristened Maggot during the war and carried that callsign to the end of his career. Maggot had been a former enlisted Marine and had gotten a commission through the Enlisted Commissioning Program. Not incidentally, his father had been an admiral in the Navy.

I absolutely respected Maggot but sometimes I also thought he lived a charmed life. A fighter pilot's eyes were of first importance and Maggot almost lost his. After getting his wings, a new Marine pilot was sent to a Replacement Air Group, or RAG, where he was trained in the airplane to which he had been assigned. The higher the pilot's class standing, the more likely he got the plane he wanted. Fighter types went to one of two bases—Yuma, Arizona, or Cherry Point, North Carolina. Attack people went elsewhere and reconnaissance and electronic warfare people, to yet other bases. KC-130 people went wherever they went. Helicopter guys had their own pipeline. We didn't much mix with them.

Maggot went to Marine Corps Air Station Yuma where the West Coast RAG was located. Once done with the RAG, he got orders to his first gun squadron based in El Toro, California, the West Coast F-4 base. Late one night while driving his Corvette, the young bachelor fighter pilot's chariot of choice, Maggot had an accident on the highway between Yuma and El Toro and landed upside down in a ditch off the side of a highway. Lucky for him some hunters found him the next morning hanging unconscious in his seatbelt, one eyeball dangling out on the optic nerve. Somehow, they got him out of the car and to a hospital where both he and the eye were amazingly saved. Not so the Corvette.

Charmed life maybe but charm had little to do with Maggot's prowess in the bird. He had, in my opinion, the best hands in VMFA-115. Totally trustworthy, taking fire or not.

Section Two—Hops

In The Rose Garden, Maggot was one of my hootchmates, along with The Fat Maggot. It got confusing that two hootchmates were Maggots and that they shared the same last name. No blood relation.

Living in very close quarters—a 15-by-20-foot hootch—we were very aware of each other's little personal quirks. Personal peccadilloes even became a source of unforgettable humor. In those days, Maggot was a smoker. His habit was to wake up, crack open a can of Coca-Cola, take a long pull and fire up a Marlboro. All that would be followed by a fit of coughing and hacking. One day when I asked him if he was going to the mess hall for breakfast, he answered, "I've already had the fighter pilot's breakfast—a Coke, a smoke and a choke." I laughed. I still laugh.

Maggot also had a fixation with shaving. In the Garden, some of us let shaving slide a day or so, especially if we had the early-early brief at 4:00 a.m. Or a light beard. But not Maggot. He shaved every day. Several mornings, I woke in a confused dream state to what sounded like active woodpeckers in the trees of my boyhood home. Ten or fifteen whacks in a row. But it was just the Maggot assiduously knocking hair out of his metal razor against the side of the plastic dish he used as a basin.

***

Maggot and I flew one particular hop out of the Garden that seemed to combine his charmed life and his exceptional skill. Although there was an eight-inch opening between the cockpits on either side of the RIO's instrument panel, it was impossible for pilot and RIO to hear each other without the mics which were housed in our helmets. The jet blast that came from the engines while flying at 500 knots was way too loud inside the plane.

To overcome the noise, the Phantom had an inter-cockpit radio system, ICS, with two modes, cold mic and hot mic. Cold mic was standard operating procedure most of the time when we were on the west side of the Mekong. Cold-mic communication required either pilot or RIO to take the step to hold down a button to talk to each other. Once we crossed the river into bad-guy country, the pilot flipped a switch allowing hot-mic or instantaneous communication between pilot and RIO. On this hop when we crossed the Mekong, Maggot tried to come up hot mic and nothing happened. No communication at all. Thinking that Maggot had forgotten to go hot mic, I stepped on my floor switch to remind him. Still nothing happened.

I looked up into Maggot's rearview mirror. He was looking back with his mask off, giving me an I-don't-know facial shrug. I gave a hand signal and mouthed that I had checked the circuit breakers. All in. I tried every

Chapter 11. Silence from the Backseat

UHF frequency, including Guard, but both my UHF radio and the ICS system were dead. From the back seat, I couldn't communicate with the front seat or out into the world.

I signaled thumbs-up or thumbs-down, asking whether we were going to scrub the hop, which we were supposed to with this kind of equipment malfunction, or press on. He communicated with his hands that we were going to go ahead, that he would do the radios and we could pass notes between the canopies. And he quickly passed the first one, shaping it into a paper airplane, which he jetted back to me. It said *Press. Can do dive. Can talk to FAC. Call mark with two bangs canopy, left side. Right side, if emergency.*

On one earlier hop with Maggot, our plane had been hit and we didn't know it until a ground handler called us back to show us the damage after we had started our post-landing walk back to the line shack. We looked at each other and Maggot said, "It just wasn't our day to buy the farm." One time a plane captain—a ground crew man—showed Maggot where a round had hit directly under his ejection seat but lacked enough energy to go farther than the skin of the plane. Maggot laughed it off saying, "I really didn't need an enema anyway."

On our failed ICS hop, I briefly considered if we should be legal and return to base or go with it. I knew the answer. I was with Maggot. I knew he had steady hands and a cool head. I looked back at him in the mirrors and gave the thumb-up. He grinned, mask off. He had a way of jogging his head up and down that communicated when something was really funny or edgy. He was laughing so I laughed too. And we pressed on with Maggot doing the talking.

I did my banging on the canopy like a champion and the hop was otherwise uneventful. We got good hits, bingoed into Da Nang, told no one except the ground crew there about our mic troubles and had the bird fixed. We flew another bombing mission on the way home, hot mic working, and we laughed about what we had done when we got back. Had the pilot been anyone but Maggot, I would have raised hell by message and voted to RTB.

***

Some sticks had what was later famously called *the right stuff*. In 1972, that phrase had not been coined but Maggot had plenty of it. He was exceptional in the Phantom. And it didn't hurt either that his life may have been charmed.

CHAPTER 12

An Award-Winning Hop

November 1972

Square was the pilot on what turned out to be an award-winning hop. He was tall, early bald, slow talking, quick witted, with good hands in the plane. Hard-headed, stubborn, aggressive in the air, single-minded and totally capable. He had wanted the callsign Rounder but that one was already taken so Round became Square. I had known Square when we were both in VMFA-312 at Cherry Point.

***

Marine flyers often had a thing about authority. It bugged them. Square was one of these authority-averse pilots and an incident at Cherry Point had only hardened him further. Our squadron had been sent a new Heavy, a major, callsign Driver, who by then had done two tours in Vietnam. He was a hard-ass.

Square had the intelligence officer job in that squadron, requiring him to keep secure all classified documents and publications. His office at the top of stairs, which everyone had to climb, featured a metal office door with double 24-inch strap-hinge braces and a huge and complicated set of locks. There were two tumbler locks with different combinations as well as a key lock. It took some serious doing to open that door.

On the day Driver arrived, he climbed to the top of the stairs where he saw Square fumbling with that lock. "All ya gotta do is be smarter than the lock, Lieutenant," Driver said as he walked off. That snide comment stuck in Square's craw. When he got to Vietnam, he grudgingly remembered that run-in with Driver's authority and did not back off his jaundiced view of any authority at all.

Square had arrived at The Rose Garden before I did. By the end of my year at the Garden, I had 36 combat hops with him and I never worried on any of them. He knew his stuff and I knew he was okay. On this particular hop, Square and I ended up in a hot area known to be heavily defended.

Chapter 12. An Award-Winning Hop

We were told to expect triple-A fire. Anti-aircraft artillery fire of several calibers.

Our target was a suspected enemy emplacement. The FAC was pretty sure there was a tank hidden under some trees in a corner of jungle. Tanks were a big deal, hard targets that could do heavy damage to our allied ground forces. The FAC talked Square's eyes onto the trees that he suspected hid the tank, fired a willie pete and adjusted us from the smoke. On our first run at the target, Square spotted the tank we would take on, probably a Russian model, and he had the FAC plenty excited.

"Pressing," Square said, as he flew on past my called release point for the first five bombs. He had a good feel for where the release point needed to be so he overrode my call. It was a trust issue and didn't happen often. "Square," the FAC responded, "you hit just off dead center on the tank. A hard but glancing blow. Bent the main barrel but the turret's still on." As we pulled up for the next run and looped around to re-enter the race-track pattern, Square cursed a blue streak. He was furious that the hit hadn't been head-on.

As we rolled in after being cleared to fire on the second run, he told me that he was going to press again. "I'm going to get that bastard." I was seeing his hard-headed aggressiveness and target fixation in spades. Square wanted that tank and I trusted him to get it without flying us into the ground. And I knew he didn't want to slam into the ground any more than I did. I made my mark call and felt the Phantom skid to one side. That small skid was Square's intuitive last-second adjustment. I felt the thumps as the last five bombs came off the bird. An inveterate hunter from the woods of Mississippi, Square knew about Kentucky windage, how to correct his aim to hit his target.

As we pulled off from the second run, I turned around to see the hits. Mostly dirt and smoke geysering in the air. The FAC dropped down to get our bomb damage assessment, which was given as a percentage of the target destroyed and other damage done. The area was quiet for a minute and then he came back on the air, more excited now. "Square, direct hit, 100-over-100! One tank destroyed. Four stacks of supplies."

The FAC couldn't quit talking. "You hit him head on, Square. You bent the tube of the tank! The turret was blown off and is lying in the road next to the tank. Really good hits! Nice work!" In the cockpit, all Square said was, "We got the son of a bitch."

***

69

The author (L) stands with pilot Square (R) beside a loaded F-4B Phantom. This aircrew flew a total of 36 *red-ink*, or combat, hops from The Rose Garden between September 1972 and March 1973, as well as many other *black-ink*, or non-combat hops, during that period. In November 1972, they got the unofficial Top Gun Award from VMFA-115 for the best Bomb Damage Assessment of the month, 100-over-100. One tank destroyed and four stacks of supplies (author's collection).

During the next week, Square and I got the unofficial Top Gun Award from the Squadron for the best BDA of the month. Neither of us ever flew against a tank again.

CHAPTER 13

Watch Dog and Beer

November 1972

On the morning of 20 November 1972, VMFA-232 pilot Watch Dog and his RIO Beer were flying a combat mission in a very hot area near Tchepone, Laos. Their plane was hit by anti-aircraft artillery fire and they were quickly in a high-speed dive, out of control. It was not their day. Both ejected immediately. Watch Dog tried to spot Beer's parachute as soon as his own opened but he didn't see it. What he did see were the gun emplacements that were still firing.

By this time, other Marine and possibly Air Force planes had come to the site. Watch Dog's chute was still in good shape, so as he descended he got out his survival radio and took on the role of a parachute-borne forward air controller, directing the bomb runs of the planes that had come to help and letting the friendlies know the location of the still-firing enemy. Both to inflict damage and to prevent another shoot-down.

Watch Dog was a big, muscular guy. I often saw him in The Rose Garden's makeshift gym doing his weight workouts and I know he was stout. Beer, as I remember, was slightly built. Their physical builds were important because it was likely that their plane was making at least 500 knots when it was hit and they punched out. That speed alone could cause major physical damage due to wind blast and limb-flail, if, in fact, the artillery rounds were not fatal.

Watch Dog hit the ground and quickly gathered up his chute. That was the very first thing we were taught to do in an escape-and-evasion situation. Get rid of the telltale parachute that could give away our position. Make it as hard as possible for the bad guys to find us. Watch Dog had taken the best bail-out information from the FAC. He began his E-and-E plan by telling the FAC and friendly Marine aircraft his direction of escape and roughly where he planned to be the next morning. He headed into the jungle to spend one very strange night.

***

71

Survival is an important word in the Marine war lexicon. It is imperative to know as much as we can about what to do if we are caught in a situation where our survival depends largely on what we know and what we do. I had attended mandatory basic survival school in the States before going to Wes-Pac and had learned the rudiments.

Later in my war career, I was ordered to a school in the Philippines with the unlikely name of JEST, Jungle Environment Survival Training. My instructor Mario, an older Filipino, had lived in the jungle during World War II and had been a resistance fighter against the Japanese. He taught us how to split a man's head with one swipe of a bolo knife, how to build traps and snares from sticks and string to catch jungle fowl, which plants were edible and which were drinkable. We had to evade unseen for about half a day.

To graduate from JEST, we were taken to a remote place in the jungle where we spent the night with the barest of necessities. Then we had to get ourselves rescued. With the use of our survival radio, we would contact the rescue helicopter in the area. We would give him a short hold-down, pressing the transmit button on the radio for about ten seconds. His receiver had the capability to point with a needle where the radio transmission was coming from and he would then fly the needle. Listening to the sound of the rotor blades, we knew the direction the chopper was flying and we talked non-stop to give the pilot a strong signal. When he was close, we asked if he wanted a flare or a smoke to identify our position. Visibility from the copter's viewpoint was paramount and would determine which signaling device we should use.

When he saw us visually—we would look like a little dot in the jungle—he flew directly over us and dropped a jungle penetrator, a long, heavy bullet-shaped device on a cable. The trick was not to let the jungle penetrator hit us. It could kill. The penetrator had metal fins that popped open after it hit the ground. We would hop on, give the pilot a thumbs up, and he would pull us up into the chopper. But that was training, not war.

***

On the ground, Watch Dog moved to where he had told the friendlies he would be the next morning. His rescue was successful. His survival training, plus his own good sense and extraordinary presence of mind, may well have saved his life on the night of 20 November 1972. Here was this guy, possibly hit, who had punched out of a crashing plane in a parachute, and had acted heroically during descent to help himself escape and keep the friendlies going after the targets. It was astounding to me that he kept himself together in those dire circumstances.

After the war, I met Watch Dog again at an impromptu VMFA-232 reunion at the El Toro, California, Officers Club. By then he had gotten completely out of the Marines and was head of the SWAT team for the Los Angeles Police Department. We talked casually some about that day but I figured it was better to leave it alone. The Marine Corps talks up physical and mental toughness. Watch Dog had both, and to spare.

***

Eight years later back in the U.S., I had gotten out of flying, then had got back in as a reservist. One of the schools I had to attend to get back into the Phantom was SERE school—Survival, Evasion, Resistance, Escape—at Marine Corps Air Station, El Toro. The currency time on my JEST training in the Philippines had elapsed as had the latest thought-to-be enemy. Vietnam was old news by then.

When the sections on *presence of mind* and *assisting in your own rescue* were taught at SERE, Watch Dog's escape was used as an example. After that class ended, I went up to the teacher and explained I was airborne nearby in Laos on that day, knew Watch Dog and some of the guys that kept fire suppressed while he escaped and evaded in the jungle. He wanted to hear what I knew. I told him I was certain Watch Dog's physical strength had made a big difference helping him survive the high-speed ejection and grueling night in the jungle. I recommended the bolo knife. From my JEST school onward, I had flown with mine strapped to my leg. And I said that whatever it took to get *presence of mind* instilled in his students might very well be the difference between life and death. As it had been for Watch Dog.

***

Friendly planes stayed on site as long as they could on 20 November, 1972, looking for Beer. I know of two examples. Branch and Batjack, a 115 air-crew, were instructed by the FAC to make as many really low and fast passes as they could over the target to keep the bad guys' heads down. They flew their unarmed Phantom straight and level over the NVA gunners, who continued to fire. Low altitude causes the Phantom to drink fuel fast but Branch and Batjack flew as long as they could, then told the FAC they really had to leave. They made it back to The Rose Garden on fumes. They were flying famished. Both Branch and Batjack were awarded the Navy Commendation Medal with Combat Distinguishing Device, or Combat V, for that hop.

Section Two—Hops

Maggot, my hootchmate, and his Section were also nearby when Watchdog and Beer were hit. Maggot, whose plane was still armed, took the risk of breaking the Rules of Engagement to fly three low-angle passes, dropping two bombs on each of the first two passes and six bombs on the third, in order to maximize the cover they could provide, giving Watchdog and Beer a better chance to escape and evade.

Maggot's tactic was unorthodox. Business as usual would have been two high-dive runs max, dropping five bombs on each pass. But Maggot made his own decision that when a Marine plane was down, he would do the most he could to help, whatever it took, and business as usual be damned. Maggot and his RIO Lighthorse were awarded Single Mission Air Medals for their efforts. The Single Mission Air Medal is a step up from the Air Medal and just below the Distinguished Flying Cross.

***

Beer was never found. What has stayed with me was that I had passed him just the morning of his death. We both said a casual, "Hey," and went off to another day in the office, our Lexan-covered cockpits. I made it back and he did not. Long after the war, I began writing a weekly newspaper column for my hometown newspaper. It has become my tradition to write about Beer every year during the week of 20 November.

Semper Fidelis, Beer. We do not forget.

Chapter 14

Night Tanking

November 1972

The order to go north came on us quickly in mid–November 1972. We had heard talk that a major operation against North Vietnam was being planned for the not-too-distant future. Rumors said it was Hanoi we'd be hitting. The amperage in the usual flow of conversational electricity around the Garden had been stepped up. *Bull's Eye*, the code name for Hanoi, could often be heard at the O-Club bar.

Going north consistently was something different for us. For one thing, it meant that we might have engagements with actual MiGs. It also meant flying against stiffer anti-aircraft artillery, more and bigger guns and more SAMs. The Rose Garden had already lost one Phantom and Marine pilot from 232 to a MiG and there was a streak of vengeance among us. I felt it.

At an All Officers Meeting, Clipper stood up, looked around and said flatly, "OK, it's on. The direction is north. We're gonna start training up." He took a breath before going on and as he continued, his eyes swept around the room. "No reason those bastards on the boat get to be the only ones that bag a MiG." By then Marines Bear and Lil' John, off the USS *America* anchored at Yankee Station, had gotten a MiG kill. Murmurs rippled through the meeting and a small barely perceptible grin crept onto almost every face in the room.

By this time, the Hanoi Hilton and what went on there was common knowledge. Any of us would have flown any mission to facilitate the escape or release of our countrymen who were missing and, we thought, might be POWs. But we had to go to North Vietnam to do that. Many of us personally knew someone whose status and whereabouts were unknown. We desperately wanted those men from The Rose Garden to be alive—Chipman, Cordova, Forrester, Kroboth, Peacock, Price, Robertson. These were men whose faces I knew and remembered, men who might still be alive. Somewhere.

We knew we had work to do to get ready including practicing missile shoots and sharpening up on RHAW gear. We had to get better at everything from navigating and tanking to mutual support tactics. Clipper continued, "We're gonna have to do some night tanking." The air went out of the room. Tanking was an unpleasant necessity at any time, but at night? Damn.

***

For my first night-tanking training hop, I was scheduled to fly in the Lead plane with Clipper himself. He was a very good stick and a pleasure to fly with but he was still the skipper. Like everyone else in the Squadron, I didn't want to let him down. When I flew with him, I wanted him to think that he was flying with the best RIO in the outfit, whether he was or not.

The tanker crews came over to our makeshift ready room in the barn the next afternoon for the brief. Refueling our planes at night would be just as challenging for them. It would require more coordination than our usual daytime plugging. Like us, they had the day routine down including some jousting when things didn't go quite right.

We had also seen the tanker crews in rough flying. Like the time we were stuck in really bad stormy weather coming back from a long hop in the daylight. We were at 30,000 feet and were having a hard time even seeing Basketball. Thank goodness for radar. We actually couldn't see him until we were very near him. Not good. But our bird was desperate for fuel and Basketball knew it. He radioed us to hold on while he found a hole in the clouds where we could tank. Problem was there was no hole. And we had another challenge. Basketball's max speed on a good clear day was close to stall speed for our birds so we had to *toboggan*, letting the KC-130 dump his nose for a long dive to gain speed so that tanking would be easier.

We hoped all that rough flying experience would prepare us for what we had to do now. We briefed on the rendezvous time, the approximate location, altitude, direction of the track and amount of give-away fuel. Then the head tanker pilot, Basketball Lead, told us how refueling in the dark would go. "This will be Emcon," he said to our surprise. Emissions controlled, Emcon, meant we would be flying with no radios or lights, a radar-only rendezvous, and then we would kill the radar. "Go nose cold, *switches safe* in Observation," he told us. Position lights and radio com could tell NVA gunners and missileers where we were.

Clipper piped up, talking directly to the tanker crew, "Hey guys, this is only training! What if we can't find you?" Basketball came back. "Tell us to turn the lights on," he said calmly. "We'll light up like a Christmas tree."

After the brief, we were uneasy as we waited for the sun to go down. We had all met the flight-time minimums for night flying in order to get flight pay and stay street legal. Rules and regs were rules and regs, war or not. But often we did the bare minimum to follow them. We might take off just before sunset and pull our green visors down but still log the flight as nighttime. *This* hop had to be done in the black dark. Part of the necessary prep for dealing with flights north and maybe MiGs.

We broke up with Basketball and briefed among ourselves, then suited up and walked to the birds with none of the usual chatter. Start, taxi, take-off and join-up, all ordinary. We drilled towards the rendezvous point. In 1972 the nighttime countryside in Thailand was devoid of electric lights. The ground was black dark with only a wispy horizon. I was working the radar in 100-mile scale when I got the faint smudge of a blip, strong enough for me to call Contact, hoping the blip was Basketball. It was.

We flew, guiding on the contact. Our Two plane got a weak tally-ho, meaning they visually saw the tanker. They made the call to Basketball and his crew. As Two made the turn towards Basketball, the silhouette of the KC-130 was distinct against the last trace of sunset. Radios were ordered silent and our position lights were turned off, as were Basketball's. Clipper crept our plane towards the tanker at about 300 knots. I was now in 50-mile-scale radar. We were closing. On my best guess, we elevated up to 1,000 feet above and drilled toward Basketball.

With the radar in ten-mile-scale, I had a good strong bogey. I knew where Basketball was. Now my job was to get Clipper's eyes on that tanker. All daylight had faded, leaving no horizon. "Ya got him?" I asked Clipper. "No joy," was the reply. "Ya got him now?" I asked again. "No!" It was also quiet from Two but this was Clipper leading the hop. Nobody would give him grief, me included.

We drilled into what I estimated to be within four miles of Basketball. "No joy," said Clipper again. He still couldn't see him. I was starting to wonder if my contact was bogus. But Clipper had a lot of radar time and he was confident my radar contact was Basketball. Son of a bitch. Clipper decided to break Emcon. We were, after all, still in Thai airspace. "Basketball, we are in Observation, no joy. Turn your lights on."

Basketball's one-line response was, "They are on." We were all in the blind. Dead silence. Then after a long minute, Two chimed in, "There he is, ten o'clock low." The lights went back off and we went nose cold again, turning off the radars, and the rest of the hop went as advertised. Clipper plugged in on the second pass. We took in the token fuel and headed back to The Rose Garden.

When they heard what had happened and checked the plane, the maintenance guys figured out that my radar set was out of calibration. Basketball had actually been 3,000 feet below us. We had been looking too high and too far ahead. We had been nearly on top of him. That's why we couldn't see him. At the debrief with Basketball, little was said but wary, accusatory looks were exchanged. We didn't tell him about the radar problem. Sounded like too wimpy an excuse.

Later at the O-Club, our Section rehashed the hop over a tall cold one, or five. No one really wanted to say anything. All of us felt stupid. Finally, old Clipper broke the silence, "Turn your lights on, I said to him. And then the son of a bitch answered, 'they are on.' I'll never forget that." None of us would. None of us had to go north at night either.

CHAPTER 15

Flying in Laos

November 1972–January 1973

Laos was important to the North Vietnamese. By 1972–1973, the NVA were seeing the end. They were heading south as fast as they could, however they could get there, with the ultimate goal of overtaking Saigon, South Vietnam. The road networks in Laos and in Cambodia, both west of Vietnam, were full of military materiel, trucks, supplies, troops, large weapons and ammunition. The NVA used every means of conveyance they could find. We had to get used to having as targets *sampans*, sandal-like flat-bottomed fishing boats, as targets, full not of fishermen but of soldiers who stood and fired at us with rifles.

We became familiar with places in Laos that had nicknames often from geographical features. Road Runner, Snoopy's Nose or the Dick in the River, this one named for a place where the Mekong made a hairpin turn, then turned back on itself in equal length. We got very familiar with places like Camp Carroll, Cam Lo, Tchepone, and *Plaines Des Jarres*. Any place in the PDJ could be counted on to be nasty.

As 1972 crawled toward 1973, the tempo of aviation operations at The Rose Garden stayed steady and even increased at times. During the months of November 1972 through January 1973, I averaged 50 flight hours a month, all red ink in my log books. During those three months, RIO's were flying their rear ends off. Everyone at the Garden did their best to keep their situational awareness sharp. The maintenance troops were worked to a frazzle but did the best they could with what they had to keep the planes in the air, safely and effectively. But that didn't always happen. We have the bad hops to prove it.

***

Early November 1972. The day started off as an edgy one, even in the brief. I had never flown with the pilot Stopper. I was relatively new and he was a Heavy with a reputation as a dot-the-i's, cross-the-t's sort of officer.

But he was a second-tour so I figured I would dot-the-i's, cross-the-t's, not take anything for granted and maybe learn something.

Start, taxi, take off were uneventful. Tanking was so-so and with little banter in the cockpits because the only Heavies we ever shot the breeze with were Clipper and Beak. Clipper, because he took more than casual interest in all of his men. Beak, because he was our maintenance officer. He needed to know the actual conditions of the planes from a crew point of view.

We came off the tanker and soon switched frequencies to our airborne-command-and-control center that handed us off to our FAC. We were headed to a hot part of Laos, heavily contested at the time, which meant defensive ground fire. We knew from the FAC's description and use of geographical features that the hop could be a tough one. He listed the weapons the enemy might shoot at us, local altimeter setting, and best bailout, which was anywhere but Laos. We gave him the line-up of the section, number and type bombs, and time on station, the amount of gas left to work with measured in minutes. We armed our bombs and switched on the five-inch Zuni rockets.

The FAC said the area had seemed surprisingly calm to him that day. Odd in this heavily contested area. He wasn't exactly sure about the specific site we were to hit. Maybe camouflaged supplies. He didn't know yet. We circled above, *switches safe*, while he attempted to mark the target, which seemed to be taking an overly long time. I started getting suspicious but said nothing to Stopper.

I had heard about flak traps, but thus far, sort of early in my war experience, I had not come across one. Stopper's experience was much more significant. He would know but he said little except that it was taking the FAC a long time to get down a good marker.

Finally, we rolled in and were cleared hot and soon saw a world of small blue puffs of smoke surround us. The blue smoke came from 23-millimeter-cannon projectiles that self-detonated at a pre-determined altitude of 14,000 feet. The 23s were familiar to us because many of them were U.S.-made and had been sold to various countries after World War II. Our plane still had to dive through the smoke to bomb so as I looked out the sides of the canopy, I called for speed and a steeper dive angle and then called *mark* to release the bombs.

I transmitted, "Flak trap, heavy," over the radio to give Dash-Two a heads up. Two told, didn't ask, the FAC, to change the run-in heading, which the FAC did, realizing what had just happened. As Stopper and I pulled up to re-enter the pattern, this time from a different heading, Stopper said, "Good call. I shoulda known." *Yeah, no shit,* I thought to myself.

The Two plane met resistance but not as heavy as we had. Stopper and I agreed to pick our own run-in heading for our second run and flew away from the target for a few seconds telling Two and the FAC what we were doing. Confuse the enemy, make them think we were hit, then come in fast and steep from an unpredictable direction.

We began the second run and this time Stopper was faster and on a solid 45-degree dive angle. The steeper the angle, the less likely the plane would be hit. As soon as we were on the dive angle, we started hosing off the Zuni rockets, which seemed to delay the fire we had been taking from all around us. Two had hosed his rockets off but we hadn't used our rockets on the first run. Now they knew we could and would shoot back. For effect and confusion, I began popping flares in the pullout in case the enemy had shoulder-fired SAM-7 missiles at us. The flares burned with a bright red glow and were hot enough to make a SAM-7 think *they* were the target, not the tailpipe of the Phantom.

Stopper and I joined up with Two, up high, flew under each other to check for bullet holes and hung bombs. No holes and a reasonable amount of gas left. Then the FAC came on. "BDA was forgettable. Few on target." "I have to admit," he said sheepishly, "I didn't know it was a trap." That day and that hop were not forgettable for me. I can say now that was the day I earned my salt. I should never take for granted that the guy in the front seat has a situation wired. If something seemed not right, it probably wasn't.

We recovered at The Rose Garden and after doing a walk-around inspection on the bird, I stood in front of Stopper, not giving one damn about experience and rank. I put my hands on my hips in an intentionally cocky-ass-attitude pose and said, "Well?" He dropped his head and said again, "I should have known." "Yeah," I responded, "but we survived it."

"Come on," Stopper said. "We'll de-brief at the Club. I'll buy. I owe you a beer." The Two crew were already there when we walked in. They had taken some rounds, small ones, but were none the worse for wear. I remember the remark from the Two RIO to his pilot. "Those guys were diving into a shit sandwich of fire." Stopper toasted my work for that day. We were alive.

***

November 1972. I was scheduled to fly with a pilot whose callsign I honestly can't remember as Wingman on a hop to southern Laos. All had gone well until it didn't. Airborne, we topped off on the Basketball tanker and headed for the Mekong, which we soon crossed. Both planes were about to test-fire chaff and flares and turn on the radar homing and warning gear.

The next thing we knew, Gallo, the Lead pilot, and his RIO Cack broke formation and elevated rapidly up to about 3,000 feet above our agreed upon altitude. Then they came down as fast as they went up. Gallo handed the Lead over to us in the Two plane, and we knew something was very wrong. As they passed below us going down, I could see that Gallo was *killing snakes* in the cockpit—that is, he was moving the stick all over the place trying to maintain control of the airplane. Cack had his head down between his legs. Though he was a salty RIO, he was heaving up whatever was in his stomach. He stayed quiet.

I took over our communications and told my pilot I was going to declare an emergency for the Section. He assented. We squawked *emergency code 77* on our transponder so that all friendly ground-based radar could see where we were. We had to get the planes headed back to home plate, The Rose Garden. ASAP. Somehow, Gallo managed to start the sick bird into a right turn to the northwest. He stayed as near us as we would let him. We were watchful for the possibility of a mid-air collision.

"Gallo, what can we do to help?" I asked. I can't remember exactly what he said but the message was, *Just get us back safely. Now.* He had his hands full. Over the air, I read the emergency checklist procedures for what we thought might be going wrong. Gallo had already done every single item on the list and the bird was still haywire. The plane would fly along straight and level for approximately three seconds. Then the nose would pitch up and the plane would climb rapidly. Three seconds later, the plane would go into a dive. On the third iteration of this erratic behavior, I could see that the wings were rocking. That could mean that the plane was in heavy buffet, which is just before a stall condition.

I worried about the bomb loads on both airplanes but knew there was a safe area near Udorn where we could dispose of the bombs on our plane without an explosion. Gallo's bombs, I wasn't so sure about. I figured out what altitudes needed to be cleared. "Clear from 9,000 to 18,000 feet, present position all the way to Nam Phong," I remember telling the controlling agency. "And notify Nam Phong what's on the way." The controlling agency rogered my communication and gave us a better heading for The Rose Garden.

My immediate concern was that we were still over Laos in a situation that was unpredictable. We had been briefed to avoid going down over Laos, above all. Extremely dangerous. I breathed a sigh of relief when we crossed the Mekong and were over friendly soil. But the problems in Gallo's airplane had not quieted down and we still had about 200 miles to go before we got back to The Rose Garden. Those were the longest twenty minutes I had flown in the war.

We pressed on and Gallo kept fighting the crazed F-4. In hindsight, I think he had found a rhythm in that very screwed-up airplane. As we approached the Garden, we could see the runway for a change. At that time of the year, visibility was often limited because the Thai were burning the undergrowth in the jungle. We slowed to approach-speed and I could see the crash crew trucks positioned to handle whatever happened on landing. I switched us up to tower frequency and reported our position. The tower had us in sight and we were cleared to land, Gallo and Cack's plane first.

Gallo landed with his bombs intact. He may have kept them aboard because the plane's bomb-release circuitry could have been involved in the electrical problem that had caused the bird to go haywire. Landing a plane loaded with bombs could be done, had been done, but doing it was a dicey proposition. Landing a loaded whacked-out plane was a real gamble but Gallo may have had little choice. His only other option may have been to eject. Whatever the case, he masterfully timed the ups and downs of the bird and using an emergency method to blow the landing gear down and locked, he landed the bird with a hard bang. My plane flew on up to the safe area, jettisoned its bombs with the *switches safe* setting on so the bombs would not detonate. Then we returned to the Garden.

Gallo was not a good bud of mine. We got along okay but he never gave me the real debrief of what was going through his mind on that hop. We had other hops to get ready for. Cack, the sturdy RIO, was not keen to talk about it very much either. That hop had put him through the wringer.

After flight ops ended for that day, I went to the O-Club bar and had a few stiff drinks. Because I hadn't had to watch two good Marines punch out over Laos, I counted it a good day, if a shitty hop. The aviation skill and real grit Gallo showed that day saved the U.S. government an aging F-4 and earned him great credit as a Marine pilot.

***

January 1973. Nacho and his RIO Kronor launched off on what was a rather routine hop out of The Rose Garden. They were the Wingman for Lead pilot Cracker. Everything was predictable on the hop until they arrived at the target in southern Laos near Saravane, an area known to be hotly contested, highly defended. By January 1973, Clipper had ordered that our squadron's Rules of Engagement include a max of two runs on any target. Nacho and Kronor got hit hard on their second run. A 23-millimeter round punched through the leading edge of the plane's left wing and detonated, leaving the left side of the fuselage riddled with holes. Since the plane's main fuel cells were in the fuselage, fuel began to leak out fast, starving the engines. After taking the hit and dropping his bombs at the target, Nacho kept the plane in the air, trying to climb and turn the wounded bird back toward The Rose Garden.

The crew of the Lead plane did everything possible to help in establishing that directional heading, making emergency broadcasts and checking for other damage. With their hands full of bleeding airplane, Nacho and Kronor focused on getting across the fence. West of the Mekong. After a flight that must have seemed likes hours but was probably less than one hour, they had The Rose Garden in sight. With no other major problems to the plane, Nacho and Kronor decided to make an arrested landing. They would use the plane's tailhook and the arresting cables at the end of the runway to stop quickly. They couldn't lower the flaps, which had been shot up and disabled, so the landing would be hot, or fast, necessitating use of the tailhook. Somehow, Nacho's excellent flying and Kronor's experience as a second-tour RIO got the airplane on the ground intact. No fire, no running off the runway. The plane was later *struck*, as the terminology went, and the parts in usable condition shipped to Japan to be parted out or put back into the supply chain.

A picture of the plane from the *VMFA-115 Silver Eagles 1972–1973 Cruise Book* shows that a flight jacket would not cover the large hole in the plane's wing. Back home after the war, I showed this picture to some World War II vets, who had taken pictures of similar damage their planes had received.

Cracker, the Lead pilot, tried to cover his ass by saying he had told Nacho to make only one run at the target, not two. He seemed to show no concern for his Wingman, only for how the incident would look on his record. When that news spread through the squadron, certain members of the bunch took it upon themselves to disassemble Cracker's bed and stick the pieces up in the rafters of the shower room, which was all the way at the other end of the company street from Cracker's hooch. I don't know of anyone who helped him get the bed down. After the war, Nacho told me that if he ever saw Cracker in civilian life, he would punch him out. I seconded that motion.

And still the story continued. Clipper decided that the actions of Nacho and Kronor rated an award. Not just any award, but a DFC, a Distinguished Flying Cross, comparable to a Silver Star. After years of perilous flying, no other aircrew in 115 had received this award. No doubt this hop took years off the lives of both Nacho and Kronor. We were all proud for them. An award well deserved.

***

I write this cockeyed confessional, which doesn't always show Marine aviation at its best, to disabuse any reader that things always went well flying out of The Rose Garden during the last year of the war. We were flying planes that been flown almost to death. They were old when we got them, had been in service since the early 1960s, often slamming on and off aircraft carriers.

Given that the F-4 Phantom II had some 63,000 parts, it was not at all surprising that things would go wrong at a given time especially when we were flying those planes in such perilous conditions. These three stories that happened over Laos suggest some of that wear and tear. Some of it didn't show up until later when I was flying in the reserves. For example, in 1975, a wing literally fell off of an F-4 over the Pacific. Two men were killed. The Phantom II wouldn't be retired until 1998.

The bad hops described here are not meant to fault our maintenance crews at The Rose Garden. Our troopers kept up two and sometimes three shifts of work day after day, month after month, living in what would now be officially declared poverty. During my year in the war, I never saw any other squadron's enlisted men work as hard and selflessly and intelligently as these enlisted men did. But it was a legitimate concern as to how they could possibly sustain the close attention their maintenance work required. Especially during periods like the intense three months from November 1972 through January 1973.

Our squadron at The Rose Garden was a motley crew with personality differences at all ranks. We didn't always get along. But we found a way. After all, we were American and all one color—*green*, as in Marine. Seniority ruled in the end. I never served in another position during my 31 years as a Marine officer where I saw seniors, both commissioned and enlisted, have to dig so deep so fast to contain volatile situations, both professional and personal.

Sometimes the outcomes of our hops were good, other times not so much. Aircrews performed feats that in any other circumstance would have earned them a Single Mission Air Medal, if not a DFC. But in a way nobody cared. Except us. The war in Vietnam officially ended in January 1973. We were told that the United States would no long officially *be* there. Marine infantry were removed. Marine aviation into North Vietnam was verboten. But the war was not over for us. We were still flying in Laos.

CHAPTER 16

The Cubi Special
Missile Shoot

November 1972

About half of VMFA-115's aircrews and planes had flown over to the Philippines, specifically to Cubi Point, for a missile-firing exercise as our combat flying was moving north to the area where a MiG could be a threat. The training records had been carefully checked and several crews were not currently certified in missile firing. Besides that, many of the aircraft needed the missile-firing circuitry certified that would put a plane in the category of *shooter*, meaning the plane could carry a missile and shoot it. For both aircrews and planes, the certification procedures had to be done.

From Cubi we would fly up to the missile-firing range off Poro Point and engage a drone, our flying target for the training exercise. When the last planes and crews arrived, Clipper passed the word we would assemble at the Cubi O-Club, in our shit-hots, at 4:00 p.m. He wanted us there in strength to show our *esprit* to the other squadrons that were there as well. After the rough in-brief on the missile exercise, we would dine together like civilized people. Before the in-brief, Clipper ordered Cubi Specials for all. On him. The Cubi Special was a potent drink, mostly rum with fruit juice of some kind in it. I thought of it as a Mai Tai on steroids.

Some background might help explain the mindset we were in on that night. For the single men especially, Cubi Point was a target-rich environment. That is to say, there were a few Department of Defense school teachers and some Red Cross workers, mostly female, who were given O-Club privileges. The women attracted crowds of men. Men who had not seen an American woman in a very long time.

There was music in the dining area and dancing later if we could find someone to dance with. Good luck with that. Clipper decided to provide his own entertainment and hoisted himself up onto his dining table and began his own personal interpretation of "Zorba the Greek," which the band was playing. Then at the musically appropriate time, he would kick a plate into the air. After a couple plates and some food went flying, the Navy officers and their wives began filing out, offended by such foolishness.

The Cubi O-Club had seen this kind of thing before. Men would come in off three-month or longer line periods on aircraft carriers and wreak havoc. The skipper of the world-famous Golden Dragons, a Navy A-7 squadron on a carrier just in from Yankee Station, was in the room that night. When he saw Clipper's performance, he did not want to be left out. He jumped up on the table, locked his arm over Clipper's shoulder and they danced and kicked as a duo. Needless to say, some damage was done but we paid the damages, went to our rooms and slept well in order to be ready to go on the real reason we were at Cubi. The missile shoot.

Next morning after the soirée, we were hung over but good Philippine coffee got us back on our feet. Very careful pre-flight inspections were performed by both maintenance and aircrews. This was a hop not to screw up by overlooking something important.

I was crewed up with the Baron, who had long ago and only once fired a Sparrow, the missile that rode the radar beam from a friendly fighter to hit an enemy target head-on. Baron really wanted to shoot a Sidewinder, the heat-seeking missile that usually hit the bogey from behind. We would try to use the Sidewinder to go against a real MiG because it was a surer shot than the Sparrow. Standard procedure was to shoot the Sparrow first, as the RIO called *Fox 1*. Then we would shoot the Sidewinder as the RIO called *Fox 2*. If we wanted to fire the Sidewinder only, as Baron wanted to do in this exercise, we would have to fake a *Fox 1* Sparrow shot, then execute a re-attack and close on our drone bogey from behind for a *Fox 2* Sidewinder shot.

To save the government money, the attacking plane was supposed to call either shot immediately upon the trigger squeeze, giving the drone driver down on the ground at Poro Point time enough to put the drone in a hard 9-G turn and defeat or escape the missile, thus saving a good drone for the next shooter. Or we could finagle the timing of the calls. If we fired the Sidewinder, we could wait a second, then call *Fox-2*. That timing allowed the missile to hit the drone and blow it up. This finagle scenario was called a *Boola-Boola*. In this case, the ground crew would launch another drone and training would continue for the next plane and crew.

Ryan, the manufacturer of the drones, didn't mind at all if we blew up their drones. They were *selling* drones. But some crews had too many *Boola-Boolas*. Chronic drone kills were frowned upon with a wry and knowing frown. Baron and I had agreed to *Boola* our drone and we did. I drove Baron to *the heart of the envelope*, the position from which we would have the very best shot at the bogey. We heard a good growl in our headsets from the Sidewinder, which told us the missile was looking dead-center at the heat source, and we had the right range, so a *Boola* we got. Baron was ecstatic and did a non-approved victory roll of our plane.

Out of five shooters that day, three scored *Boolas*. That night at Cubi's O-Club, we met downstairs in a part of the club that had been wrecked so many times it was basically bare concrete. There wasn't much that we could do to it if we got wild and crazy again. But Clipper wanted to keep things toned down after the scene the night before. We toasted the *Boola* pilots with Cubi Specials and the skipper said in his best second-lieutenant-way of speaking for us to knock off the *Boola-Boolas*, smiling as he said it. Then in his lieutenant-colonel voice, he said the last thing he needed after the previous night's mischief was to have to do a *rug dance* in front of some Navy Admiral about the condition of his airplanes. He didn't want to have to fudge that the missile-firing circuitry might have been faulty.

After the Cubi Special toasts, we decided to compensate for little or no hell to raise. We would simply see how many chairs we could stack on the newest member of the squadron. He had been a collegiate swimmer and was stout. Once the pyramid was built, the newbie was then challenged to get out from under it. He started breast-stroking out from under the chair pyramid and emerged unscathed to a standing ovation. We didn't rearrange the chairs but we did put them all back upright.

Next day, five more planes and crews shot. There was only one *Boola-Boola* and no one said a word. That afternoon, the first Section of birds left for The Rose Garden. Back to mud, crud, and bomb hops. But everyone felt more confident and had renewed faith in what the Phantom could do when used properly. And every man who went had released a certain amount of steam. As I write this, it all comes to mind as clearly as if it happened last night.

On a trip I took back to Cubi Point in 2000, I was part of an entourage that included a U.S. Senator. We stayed in the old Cubi Point bachelor officer quarters, BOQ, by then a four-star hotel. The Senator asked me what it was like at Cubi during the war. He had not served in any military capacity when Vietnam was on. I thought it best not to give too many details. I just grinned and said it was great.

CHAPTER 17

The MiG Mystique

December 1972

From the time most Vietnam aviation Marines were small boys, we knew who the American aces were in World War II and Korea. Those fighter pilots who had shot down, or *killed*, at least five enemy airplanes. Every Marine knew about Pappy Boyington, Robert M. Hanson, and Joe Foss, who holds the Marine World War II record for enemy aircraft *kills* with 26. We even knew about some of the enemy aces like Germans Manfred Von Richthofen and Adolf Galland and Saburo Sakai from Japan.

Marine fighter pilots and fighter RIOs at The Rose Garden had a dream—deep-rooted in the culture of Marine aviation—of their Phantom engaging with and shooting an enemy plane, diving and turning in the air as they shot down the plane with a Sidewinder missile. The enemy plane in the Vietnam War was generically called the MiG, manufactured in the Mikoyan-Gurevich factories, whose starting letters gave the plane its name. Mikoyan-Gurevich built a worthy adversary in the MiG-21. But if an earlier model MiG-19, -17 or -15 showed up, that would be okay too. A kill was a kill. All of them were MiGs. The North Vietnamese Air Force flew all of these models, some actually made in Russia and some in communist China, both allies of the North Vietnamese.

Knocking down any MiG would elevate a Marine aircrew to the top of the Marine jet fighter aviation hierarchy. Star status for at least five years, maybe longer. Promotion to the next rank almost guaranteed.

Since the start of the war, the Air Force had a dismal kill ratio compared to that of the Navy, of which Marine Corps aviation is a part. To further improve the Navy's kill ratio, the Navy set up Navy Fighter Weapons School, aka Top Gun, in the late 1960s, where bona fide MiG-killer pilots and RIOS were part of the instructional staff. The Navy's MiG kill dominance became even greater. As part of the Navy, Marines could go to Top Gun, making the desire to get that MiG kill even sharper. I went in 1982, long after the Vietnam era.

Chapter 17. The MiG Mystique

My Marine squadron was officially designated a fighter/attack squadron. Fighting meant engaging in air-to-air warfare. Attacking meant bombing. In reality, VMFA-115 had a hybrid mission, unlike the true attack aircraft squadrons whose planes were designated simply A for attack, meaning bombing or gunnery, i.e., the A-6s and the A-4s. VMFA-115 spent about 98 percent of our flying time in the attack mode. Marine doctrine identified 115 as a support arm for Marine infantry and any other allied or friendly infantry on the ground. But by the time I arrived in Southeast Asia, Marine infantry had been pulled out of Vietnam, as had Army infantry. We assisted allied ground forces but we never knew for certain who they were. All across the theater, we heard about the Hmong but we never met any of them. Maybe we were helping the Hmong on the ground.

When we weren't helping out our own, we did tactical attack flying to bomb designated targets the NVA needed as they made their way south. It was no secret what they were up to by then. We bombed roads, rivers used for moving supplies and troop floating, supply dumps, big artillery guns, and troops. And we were good at all of that. But we weren't engaging in air-to-air combat. We weren't really fighting. We weren't doing what we had trained to do and what we had always dreamed of doing.

This dream of a MiG kill was clearly fueled by history and culture. And by the anti-communist feelings that swirled around the 1960s and 1970s. The communists were, after all, our sworn enemies. Maybe, truth be told, some of the fuel also came from testosterone and machismo. Just a tad from a Marine aviation inferiority complex. Just before I arrived, The Rose Garden had lost a Marine F-4 from another squadron, which was shot down by a MiG. We wanted to even the score.

We were the last Marines in combat in Southeast Asia. It mattered that we got a MiG. It mattered. We didn't know then that our time would almost be forgotten in the history of the war.

***

To get to a MiG we were supposed to follow a set procedure. We first had to have a *vector*. We had to be ordered by the senior controlling agency—there were at least three in the Southeast Asia theater—to turn to a given heading, punch off or jettison the plane's external gas tanks, go *buster* in full afterburner to maximize the plane's speed, and *elevator* to a given *angels*, or get the plane up to a certain altitude. The controlling agency would then give the number of bandits and indicate the model of the plane with a color code—for example, *five blue bandits have departed from Gia*

Lam or another enemy airport. Each MiG model had a different color code. Just how the controlling agency knew this detailed information so quickly remained a classified mystery for a long time. We just knew that the agency knew.

At that point, the adrenaline was flowing. We could be cleared to engage in a fight and we knew inherent in that communication was clearance to bring down the MiG. *Judy*, the attacking RIO would say when he had the enemy plane on his radar and was in control of the fight. That's code *for I have all the info I need. I've got it.* The controlling agency then went silent unless the RIO lost contact with the bandit. *Tally-ho*, the RIO would communicate to his pilot, or vice versa, when either had a visual sighting of the bandit, when he saw it with his own eyes.

Fighting a MiG meant using the missiles we routinely carried on our planes. Firing either the state-of-the-art expensive Sparrow (approximately $400,000+ in 1972) or Sidewinder missile (approximately $200,000+ at that time) was not just an aim-and-squeeze proposition. We tried for the *heart of the envelope* so that the missiles would have their best chance to do what they were designed and built to do.

Many pilots and RIOs had arrived in-country not really ready for prime time. Bombing was covered by on-the-job training but successfully firing missiles in an air-to-air fight required specialized preparedness. Our squadron had already participated in a missile exercise in the Philippines to get us ready. The stakes could not have been higher.

The MiGs were up north, mainly near Hanoi, which we called *Bull's Eye*. The Rose Garden was in Thailand, to the south. Seldom did the MiGs stray south because they were *short-legged* airplanes. They didn't carry enough gas to fly south to fight and then return to bandit country in the north. Nor did they have tanker support like we did with our KC-130s.

The squadron ops officer assigned the daily flight schedules, determining what crews and planes flew where and when. The squadron's senior officers—the CO, XO and department heads—got first dibs on the hops going north, as maybe it should have been. The junior officers who had been most successful based on their flight experience in Nam Phong and before got the next bunch of north assignments. Everybody else got what was left on that schedule. Some guys didn't like to think of that possibility but for most we welcomed the chance. It was what we had signed up to do.

For a period of a week or so in December 1972 as our planes got close to Hanoi, we flew through a missile-heavy area—sometimes as many SAM calls as one every five to ten minutes, though the number decreased over the days to maybe one per hour. The North Vietnamese were shot out. Regardless of the number and frequency, the SAM calls kept us tight in the straps. Those missiles were aimed at us and could bring a plane down.

The ignominious name for the mission of Marine F4s going north was *post-strike refuel escort*. Doesn't sound very glamorous. Certainly not as glamorous as fighting a MiG.

When we got near Hanoi, we moved into a CAP, a combat air patrol. We flew in a race-track holding pattern, making big loops as we waited to be needed to fight off MiGs that might attack our B-52s or the KC-135 jet tankers used by the Air Force. Bombers and tankers had almost no defenses built into them except a tail gun in the B-52s, or BUFFS, an acronym for Big Ugly Fat Fuckers (or euphemistically Big Ugly Fat Fellows). And to use its tail gun, a BUFF would have to be approached by the MiG directly from the rear, which was unlikely to happen. We were there to do what we could. Didn't matter. This assigned job put us up near *Bull's Eye*. If an enemy plane tried to jump a tanker or bomber, we were in business.

***

One afternoon after normal operations, we were playing combat volleyball in the company street that ran between the hootches. Earlier that day, word had spread through the Garden that pilot Beak and RIO Lighthorse had gotten a *vector* for an air-to-air fight with a MiG. We saw them shuffling toward us at the head of the dirt street. The game stopped as they approached. I could tell from the look on Lighthorse's face it had not gone well. He looked as if he could break into tears at any minute.

Beak and Lighthorse were Lead in a Section of F-4s that were part of a CAP near Hanoi. Beak and Lighthorse were the closest friendlies to an Air Force F-4 with a MiG on its tail giving chase. The friendly plane was somehow in trouble. Probably a straggler from a strike package, low on fuel, headed south for safety with just enough gas to get back home or maybe to a tanker, definitely not enough fuel to turn and burn in a dogfight with the MiG.

Beak and Lighthorse had visual contact on the friendly F-4 as it flew directly overhead. Almost immediately, the chasing MiG turned back to the north and executed his own *bug-out*, or hasty retreat. The MiG probably saw the threat that Beak and Lighthorse were making and it was probably low on fuel as well. Lighthorse had the MiG locked up on his radar. The controlling ground agency had already given Beak and Lighthorse the vector. They had received their heading, and the order to arm their missiles, jettison their external fuel tanks, if needed, and maximize their speed up to the MiG's altitude.

Up they went, armed and fast. But before Beak and Lighthorse got close enough for a tally-ho, the controlling agency emphatically ordered them to *knock it off,* cease the intercept. Return to the CAP and orbit. Not sure why. The entire U.S. strike force headed home to the planes' various fields. As far as Beak knows, no other airborne plane got a vector for this bandit on this day. But Beak and Lighthorse *had* received an actual vector for a MiG. Much coveted. At least our guys got to go into the arena. The rest of us continued to dream.

***

Beak was a Heavy by then and a very good Marine officer and pilot. On this day, he followed orders as most good Marine officers did and do. He was told to break it off and he did. He did the right thing, which most of the rest of us, cocky as we were, probably would have done as well. We were all taught to follow orders.

But it was hard for him, for us, to lose this chance, and we all vowed silently that if we were ever again given a vector and had a lock-up or a tally-ho, we'd do what it took. Fake a radio malfunction or a garbled transmission to take it to a fight and get a kill. Screw ground control. Probably false bravado but that's what we told ourselves.

For more than forty years, I held on to what turned out to be a false story about this almost-got-a-MiG day. That the controlling agency vectored an Air Force Section right in front of Beak and Lighthorse. That we got shafted, we got robbed. Turns out that version was just a rumor, maybe a way to make ourselves feel better. But the whole episode does indeed show the mystique of the MiG.

CHAPTER 18

The Bunker

December 1972

On 13 December 1972, I spent my first full night in-country, actually in Vietnam. By then I had already flown 40 combat missions in the Phantom but I had spent only a little ground time in Vietnam proper.

According to the flight schedule, on this day my pilot Bantam and I were going to Da Nang for a turn-around. We were to take off from Thailand, do an aerial refueling event, fly a combat mission, and recover in Da Nang. We would debrief, refuel, rearm, eat, rebrief and take off again, doing another combat mission on the way home to Nam Phong. The Da Nang turn-around. Not unusual. During our flight mission to Da Nang, we met with some strong resistance over the target. The rounds shot back at us made blue puffs when they self-detonated at about 14,000 feet. We could see them. Many large bullets we had to dodge.

The rough hop into Da Nang became an overnight stay because our plane malfunctioned. At two o'clock that afternoon, we were down, in the maintenance sense. The plane had blown a tire on landing. The wheel ended up grinding itself into the wheel brake as the brake locked and the plane skidded. Listening to the noise and feeling the plane skid, Bantam and I held our collective breath and ground our teeth. It was a close call but not all that uncommon. Our squadron was short on tires. We were at the tail end of a very long supply chain. We had all been told to get as many landings as possible out of each set of tires. Clearly, we had pushed that direction as far as possible and a little further. The good news was we weren't on fire and had suffered no actual damage. We thought.

We were stuck in Da Nang until our wheel could be replaced. The ground crew there tried all of the usual approaches to bumming replacement parts. We had a loans-and-borrows system with a sister Marine squadron stationed on an aircraft carrier out on Yankee Station. We would also beg parts from any Air Force outfit that flew the same model planes or even similar models. But this time, we couldn't turn up a replacement wheel in an hour's time. Even with The Rose Garden's promise to get us a new wheel by eleven o'clock that night and the ground crew's confirmation they would get it on the plane as soon as the parts arrived, we knew that we wouldn't be fixed and ready to fly until the following morning.

We wouldn't *want* to fly until morning anyway. The Rose Garden was barely operable in the daylight. Even then we needed clear skies. Rain usually killed the expeditionary electronic navigational aids, leaving us to rely on dead-reckoning navigation, which can't be used on a night when there are no stars, no moon and no ground light. The darkness was its own force to be reckoned with in Vietnam, Laos and Cambodia.

Heading into the debrief, Bantam said to me, "I'm not trying to land on a night this dark, new tires or not. I say we lie to Ops if we have to." I agreed. We were hungry, tired and dirty. We stunk of fear-sweat, which is different from the sweat of athletic exertion—more primal and sour, full of warning. I wanted a shower, a real shower with hot water, and I knew in Da Nang such showers could be had. It would be my first real bathing experience with hot running water in a month.

The first thing we did after debrief was head to the Red Dog Saloon in what passed for a Navy Officers Club. It was equipped with a varnished plywood bar, plain chairs and a shuffleboard table. A Navy pilot seemed to be in charge. It was only three in the afternoon but that didn't stop us from ordering large whiskeys. Inside the Red Dog was one of our jarhead Warrant Officers, Gunner, who ran the turn-around crew. He had just come off duty and was busy losing himself in a gin and tonic. He was at the point in drinking where he was starting to lower his defenses and decompress from his own day's troubles. He knew our story.

"Don't worry," he said. "You may as well stay here for the night. I already got you rooms at the BOQ. The mama-sans all left the base at two today. I figure that means rockets tonight, probably from Rocket Ridge, the usual." He paused to take another sip. "Your rooms are on the other side. I put some 782 gear in there," he said, meaning he had provided us with flak jackets and helmets. We carried our own sidearms.

In the head at the Red Dog, there was a diagram right above the urinal with directions on how to get to the bunkers. I thought I should start to ask questions while I was still sober enough to remember which direction I needed to go. I sidled back over to Gunner. "My first night in-country," I said. "Rockets? How will I know when to go to the bunker?" Gunner looked at me as if he were my wise old uncle and said with a sardonic smile, "Oh, you'll know. And sleep with your heater and ammo."

Chapter 18. The Bunker

Da Nang, South Vietnam, from outside the MAG-15 gate in November 1972 when the author was about to spend his first night in-country. This part of Da Nang was nicknamed *Dog Patch*. Rocket Ridge, seen in the background, was the frequent site of both incoming and outgoing rocket attacks (author's collection).

Bantam came back to the table with news from Ops that one of the Thai mess workers had blown up the Nam Phong field kitchen. The only food back at The Rose Garden was C-rats, heating optional. Instead, I got to eat half of Bantam's store-bought roast beef sandwich. Bantam's plan was to eat, listen to the Armed Forces Network Radio—a luxury we had only sporadically in Nam Phong, then hit the rack. Bantam was on his second tour. Rockets wouldn't keep him from sleep.

I won some money playing shuffleboard, had three more drinks and found my way to the BOQ. It was a simple wood-frame building within a walk of the flight line and the Red Dog. It turned out to be just as plain and basic as the Officers Club but even so it was way better than our hootches in The Rose Garden. I showered, guiltlessly running all the hot water I wanted. In a real room, a real bed was waiting for me with clean sheets, a real pillow and a green blanket covering a thick mattress.

I shucked off my flight boots but decided to sleep hairy buffalo in my flight suit. I was used to the smell, which had by this time lost its tinge of fear and had turned into common human stink. I kept remembering Gunner's cryptic response when I asked him how I would know when to go to the bunker. I didn't understand what *Oh, you'll know* meant but something told me it would be good to be ready for anything.

I lay down on top of the blanket, unwilling to put my filthy flight suit between clean sheets. Even the sheets and real mattress couldn't relieve me of my wartime tendency to expect the worst, and soon. And this expectation caused my eyes to open reflexively too often to allow for restful sleep so I lay there with eyes open, wondering about everything, about nothing. It did no good to dwell on anything for too long. Things could change in milliseconds. Finally, the tidal surge of cumulative whiskey consumption took over and I nodded off.

Sometime later, I was jerked awake by hard compressed sound waves that reverberated all through my body. It was as though I hadn't rested at all. I heard and felt short bass-toned whumps and their echoes. All around me, the BOQ itself was quiet but then for all I knew I was the only soul in it. The rhythmic booming sounds continued and seemed to be drawing ever closer as though NVA gunners were walking artillery rounds toward the flight line. I began to pick up on background noises, voices, not loud but serious.

Then the explosions became louder. I lay there waiting for some sense of urgency. Gunner had said that I would know when to head for the bunker. An explosion came much closer than the others and the strong reverberations throughout my body told me I *did* know. It *was* time. I sat up, put on my boots and flak jacket, grabbed my pistol and headed down the hall towards the stairs that led to the bunker. I was moving as fast as I could and still look cool, just in case I saw anyone else.

At the bottom of the stairs, a low light showed me the opening of the bunker and I scooted into a pure black hole edged by sand bags. I turned to press my back to the far wall of the bunker, realizing that I was the only person in it. The place was oddly quiet. Outside, the deep concussions continued, muffled now by the bunker walls. I rechecked my pistol. Loaded. I had 50 rounds of spare ammunition sewn in clips to my zoom bag. I waited, figuring surely at least one other American would join me, but I kept the muzzle of the pistol pointed towards the mouth of the bunker, just to be safe.

My watch showed I'd been in the bunker for five minutes, then ten minutes, then fifteen. I moved closer to the opening, the noise increasing as I neared the passageway. The rounds were still whumping with regularity and then they just stopped. Twenty minutes after I entered the bunker, all noise, all sound had stopped. I carefully peered out of the entrance. I saw the lights that had dimly lit my way were still burning. I heard voices, American voices, sounding serious but still not urgent. Ahead I saw the hall lights come on again in the BOQ. I warily made my way out of the bunker and back into the hallway toward my room.

Weaving his way down the hall with a belly full of gin was Gunner. I called out to him. He turned around slowly, looking puzzled. "What are you doing still up?" he asked.

"I'm coming back from the bunker," I said. "You know how I asked you this afternoon how I would know when to go to the bunker and you said I'd just know? You were right! About twenty minutes ago, I did know but nobody else was out there. Do you guys have another bunker, or what?"

"You mean you've been holed up because of that racket?" Gunner asked.

"Well, yeah," I said, realizing what had seemed threatening to me was apparently no big deal to an old-timer like Gunner. I started to rethink my retreat to the bunker. Maybe the enemy were known as such bad shots that old-timers like Gunner didn't worry about their rockets. I must have over-reacted. Then again, it wasn't like I was an old-timer.

Gunner's response was worse. He smiled a wide grin and said, "That wasn't *incoming*. That was *outgoing*. That was *us* shooting at the rocket boys up on the ridge. *Our* battery is right over there." He gestured toward the area where the loudest noises had come from and continued, "We're used to it."

Still grinning, he went on, "By the way, we found what messed up that wheel of yours. A spent round, probably an AK-47, punched a hole in the gear door of the wheel, shredded it. Didn't hit any hydraulic lines though. You're lucky SOBs." He turned and wove his way down the hall towards his bunk. On his way he called over his shoulder, "They're working on your plane now and we're launching you guys at eight tomorrow, right after breakfast. I'm hitting the rack. Should be a good night for sleeping. Our arty hit Rocket Ridge spot on. No rockets tonight!"

With a laugh, he disappeared into his room.

CHAPTER 19

Frags

December 1972

During the hard part of the Vietnam war, *frag,* along with its cognates, had several definitions. It could mean intentionally killing or injuring a friendly, someone on our side. Someone, for example, might have pulled the pin on a grenade and rolled it under his victim's bed and then run. Maybe as an attempt to kill a person of higher rank or authority who was thought to be dangerous or was hated by the fragger. Another motivation might have been strained race relations.

A second meaning in aviation was harming your own airplane by flying through the shrapnel pattern resulting from your own bomb.

But there's another more ordinary meaning of *frag.* A literal fragment or piece of exploded bomb or rocket. A piece of shrapnel. Two frags of this sort are part of my Vietnam memorabilia. I keep them in my Marine Corps jewelry box along with dog tags, old name tags, rank insignia and the actual pair of wings I was awarded in January 1971. One of these fragments is from a Russian or Chinese communist B-22 rocket. It is small, flat and thin, rusted brown. The second—shinier, heavier, and potentially much more wickedly destructive—is from a U.S. Mark 82 500-pound bomb. A slick.

***

In December 1972, my pilot Square and I were parked in the fuel pits at Da Nang, *hot refueling* after a Rose-Garden-to-Da Nang turn-around mission. Standard operating procedure required a plane's engines to be shut down during refueling to avoid fires. For combat expediency, VMFA-115, however, had okayed hot refueling—while the engines were running. On this particular day in Da Nang, Square and I were launching on another hop in an about an hour, so we were hot refueling.

Another reason to disconnect planes from the pumps during a refuel was that in Da Nang an airplane on the ground hooked to a fuel pump made an excellent target for North Vietnamese rockets. Those rockets could attack from anywhere at any time, as Square and I were to find out on that December day. Without warning, the attack began. Our ground troopers quickly unhooked the fuel hose from the plane and with frantic hand signals indicated a rocket attack was underway. They motioned to close the canopies and get out of there fast. Square and I had not heard the sounds of the incoming rockets above the roar of our own engines but the ground crew—their headsets tuned to a different communication channel—did hear. A B-22 rocket had hit an Air Force F-4 which was hard-down, or badly broken, and parked in an adjacent revetment, probably because the manpower was lacking to fix that plane right away. The enemy rocket exploded 100 feet and two thick concrete-and-steel walls away from where our plane was parked.

Our canopies were open and the plane's left side was parallel to the walls that separated the pit from the revetments, designed to at least partially protect broken planes from artillery, rockets, bombs or explosives. Those walls kept our plane from catching the full force of the rocket blast. But before we could close the canopies and get going, our cockpits filled with dirt, smoke and blast debris. Like a wild man, Square taxied out the F-4, while I tried to clear my clobbered eyes. After the *all clear*, we taxied back to re-arm. One of the ground crew came up to my rear cockpit with a fragment of a B-22 in his hand. "Sir," he said, "I'm sure you want a souvenir."

During that rocket attack with all the crud flying around, something lodged in my left eye, on the side closest to the blast. Twenty years later an eye doc at Carswell Air Force Base hospital told me I had a pterygium in that eye. He described a pterygium as a mass of thickened conjunctiva on the eyeball, covering part of the cornea and causing blurred vision. I called it a poor man's cataract. After a successful operation, I asked the doc what had caused the pterygium to develop. He showed me a tiny sliver of iron that had embedded in my eye. He had removed it and he offered it to me as it rattled around in a steel surgical pan. I did not save that iron sliver but I still have the frag from the explosion that sent it my way. And I still have the pterygium. Not the best kind of souvenir.

***

My second frag story requires some background. On day-to-day bombing hops, we usually flew by visual flight rules, VFR, which was fine when the sky was clear and a million because we could see our targets. But on some days during the monsoons, the weather became so overcast we couldn't see the ground. When the cloud ceiling was low and thick, it prevented

An F-4 flying straight and level as part of a *sky puke* formation over Laos. When the cloud ceiling was low and thick, six to eight Navy, Marine or Air Force planes would collect in a V-formation around an Air Force LORAN bird and all would release their bombs at the same moment on the target below. A similar *sky puke* resulted in an accidental bombing of the U.S. base at Da Nang, South Vietnam, in December 1972. Note the open *chaff* door just above the e in Marines on the side of the plane (*VMFA-115 1972–1973 Silver Eagles Cruise Book*).

any sight of the target. There was no way a plane could dive, release its bombs and recover without putting the plane and the aircrew in danger and probably missing the target anyway. At times like that, the FAC controlling us handed us off to what we called a *sky puke.*

Unlike Marine F-4s, some Air Force planes were equipped with a navigation system called LORAN, long-range aid to navigation. LORAN birds could be very precise in *seeing the target* through thick overcast by means of geographical coordinates. The Air Force controlling agency located near Da Nang would send up a LORAN bird that would troll around until six or eight Navy, Marine or Air Force birds were flying in a V-formation off its wings, like a bunch of geese. The LORAN plane would fly us to a known enemy area, get lined up on the target and make the run, straight and level. Then on his signal, all the *geese planes* would release their bombs at the same moment, split up and recover back at their ship or base.

This was a mini arc lite. A real arc lite involved at least three BUFFs, flying abreast and either in trail or in an arrowhead formation, straight and level, over a known hot area, all dropping all their bombs at the same time.

A real arc light was a frightening tactic for anyone on the ground beneath it. A B-52 fully loaded was imposing and could rattle the ground ten miles out. Three of them was a nightmare. Six to eight fighters carrying ten bombs each was nothing compared to a loaded B-52, much less three of them. But it was lethal enough.

On this particular December day, a LORAN bird and its geese were flying near Da Nang, ready for a sky puke. Meanwhile, Square and I were flying south down the coast to recover at Da Nang after our own hop up north near Quang Tri, Vietnam. We were low on fuel so I radioed Da Nang tower for landing instructions and a frantic South Vietnamese controller alerted, "Wave off, wave off, Da Nang under attack."

Along with other planes trying to land at Da Nang, Square and I decided to hold over nearby Half Moon Bay at a max-conserve fuel setting until the all-clear sounded. But all this time, gas was burning. After two turns in the pattern, Square finally yelled to me from the front cockpit, "Hell, I'm landing on a taxiway. Not gonna shitcan a perfectly good airplane." He broke out of the pattern and lined up on the outside taxiway at Da Nang.

Just then, Da Nang tower came on the air with an American controller

Silver Eagle Lead plane flying south to land in Da Nang. This photograph was taken by the author from the Wingman plane of his Section, November 1972 (author's collection).

and told us by our plane's call sign what order to land in. We were second in the emergency fuel pattern and landed without event, even made it to the fuel pits without flaming out. Our engines didn't stop because we were out of fuel. When we got to the fuel pits, our troopers were all in flak jackets and steel helmets with M-16s slung over their shoulders. But they were cheerful and even laughing.

To the north, tall plumes of thick black smoke were visible. We topped off, parked and went to ask the troops what had happened. The plane captain handling our bird said, "Sir, you won't believe it. Some Air Force jerk bombed the base." He pointed at a bucket that had steam coming out of it. He was returning from the fuel farm that had been bombed. He asked me, "Do you want a frag from the day we bombed ourselves?"

The frag I picked up was still hot to the touch. A few minutes later at the debrief on our hop to the north, an Air Force intel guy told us what had happened. The Air Force *wizzo,* or Weapons Systems Officer, in the back seat of the LORAN bird, had gotten his base and target coordinates mixed up. He entered the Da Nang base coordinates in the target window and the friendly Da Nang base became the target of the sky puke. No casualties but an embarrassing hickey for the Air Force. Forty-four years later I learned that a close friend who was *in the girls next door* F-4 squadron at The Rose Garden was one of the geese in that sky puke.

CHAPTER 20

One Wild Ride

January 1973

The highest-ranking officer permanently serving in The Rose Garden had the callsign Joker. He was our Clipper's boss, a bird colonel. We would do almost anything to protect Clipper and *not* disrespectfully calling his boss by nickname or callsign was one of those things. At least we didn't call him Joker to his face.

Joker was the CO of Marine Air Group 15 and he flew with all his subordinate units. By the time I was scheduled to fly with him in January 1973, I was salty—hard-edged, experienced. I had flown enough hops in the Phantom by then that the flight scheduler had listed me as mission commander, meaning I had overall responsibility for the safe conduct of the mission. I took the assignment as a mixed blessing. I was good enough to be mission commander and seasoned enough to be put in the Group CO's back seat. Clipper knew that I would not embarrass the Silver Eagles. In general, though, I felt unlucky to have to fly with our heaviest of Heavies.

Of course, none of this mattered to the guys we were going up against. The enemy knew nothing about hops and who was flying them. They had no idea a full colonel was in one of the two birds about to drop bombs on them. Before the flight, we briefed as usual. With the Colonel on the flight, we paid special attention when we briefed to being street legal, dotting i's and crossing t's. We made sure to double-check the familiar things we often just skipped for time's sake. As part of the briefing, we covered our expected rendezvous with an airborne tanker to refuel early in the hop.

As we started to suit up, Joker pulled me aside and said, "Look, Fleet. I am not good on the tanker. Talk to me, get me in. I can bomb okay but it has been a long time since I tanked and I wasn't very good at it then."

"Sure, sir," I replied. I knew damned good and well he was the boss of all our bosses. The only bird colonel permanently stationed at Nam Phong.

"You're mission commander, so you're the boss. Once we get in the air, drop the sir." He went on, "It's better to call me Joker."

I answered, "Yes, sir." He looked at me and smiled that gap-tooth smile he was known for. He was a big man, knew his power but also knew how to be fair. And he was smart. As I suited up that day, I told myself that Joker was just being modest about his abilities. He was just finding a way to let me know indirectly that he was good to go without preening, that I didn't need to be rank conscious.

I did the preflight inspection to show that Clipper had taught me well. The start-up, taxi and takeoff were all uneventful. Once the Mekong River was in sight, we were to rendezvous with the refueling tanker. I spotted the KC-130, its two baskets trailing in the airstream, one on either side of the tanker. Two fighters would plug into those baskets within minutes of each other and the fuel would flow. The Two plane topped off first, backed out and went in trail nearby to wait.

In the Lead plane, Joker and I had approached the tanker and I had given our position, Observation, the first position for fighters in the refueling process. It meant our plane was 1,000 feet in trail, 1,000 feet off to one side and 1,000 feet above or below the tanker. Then the tanker would clear us for the Stabilized position, 50 feet behind the basket trailing in the air stream.

"Putting the probe out," Joker said from the front cockpit. There had been no problems getting us into the Stabilized position, though over the inter-cockpit system I could hear Joker's breathing, which had become loud and rapid. I told myself that he was just an old man. I made the call to Basketball, "Stabilized starboard."

"Cleared to plug," Basketball answered. We were cleared to start trying to connect to the tanker. Plug in. That's when I found out Joker had not been showing false modesty when he told me he could not tank. We had been cleared to plug. The tanker was waiting but Joker wasn't moving.

"Talk to me," Joker said. I could hear the anxiety in his voice. Usually a pilot knew the RIO would talk. I didn't need reminding. What he meant was that he wanted me to spoon-feed him. Damn.

"OK," I said, working to keep my voice matter of fact. "Slow up. Line up just below the basket, one foot down, Joker." I could still hear his breathing and it wasn't sounding any better. "Take it a little to the left. Hold it right there." Without a pause I went on, "Now, it's at one o'clock, one foot. Make your move up and to the right and go in."

I had flown with some of the best at refueling in the squadron. The really good pilots could refuel on their own, didn't want help. They seemed to almost nudge the bottom of the 24-inch basket and jump the plane up with a stab on the first try. The F-4 had the tip of the probe to the pilot's right. Joker would have to turn his head to see it. I wanted the pilot looking at the tanker, not looking at the probe. It was more important to keep a safe interval on the several-hundred-thousand gallons of fuel traveling at 230 knots. A good RIO could talk a pilot in so the pilot could keep his eyes on the tanker.

Joker overdid the call. He was nervous and jerky. Unsure. He hooked the basket and went too far up, twelve feet up, fast. It felt like a rodeo ride. He went high enough that I saw the wing of the KC-130 underneath us. Not good. The probe glanced off the basket in a miss. That shook Joker up pretty badly. I got him back down and worked to get him calm. His breathing rate had tripled. Talking to him wasn't that easy because despite what he'd told me, Joker was still my boss's boss. I was thinking *He's a colonel!* He has to have done this in F-4 Js, F-8s and who knows what else. *He is a colonel.* You, Lieutenant, cannot give him a hard time about screwing this up. And then he screwed up again.

He missed a second time, running low under the tanker wing. I was becoming very aware that it was possible we might have a mid-air collision with the tanker. That thought superseded any other. "Nose down," I said sharply to Joker from cold-mic. To the tanker, I broadcast, "Disengaging. Re-attempt."

Hearing my tone, Basketball asked if there was a problem. My reply was a calm, cool "Negative." I was determined our flight was going to sound good even if it didn't look good.

"Back up," I said to Joker. "Back away from the basket and settle down. Right now. Then ease back up to Stabilized and sit there." I was in the air-crew mode now. I no longer cared that Joker was Group CO. We were going to do this and to hell with being polite and respectful. I had been in this situation before with a hapless major and many captains. From here on out, Joker was a lieutenant, same as I was. I would sort it out on the ground if I had to.

He sensed my change in attitude immediately, responding, "I wasn't lying, Fleet. I'm shitty around the tanker." I don't remember what I said, something to the effect of *I've seen worse.* And it was true. He was bad on the tanker and I had seen worse.

"Just stop rushing it, Joker," I said. "Settle down. We can do this."

Our Wingman in the other plane that day had already stabbed at the basket once and missed it. Two stabs and a hit were not shameful. "Do exactly what I tell you to do and not one fucking thing more. Give me one, right now." That meant to pull the throttle back one percent and he did. His breathing slowed a little. Maybe using the word *fucking* had a calming effect on old Joker. "Now Joker, you talk to me," I said. "How are you doing? You got your shit together?"

He laughed in response. "You just keep the calls coming."

"OK, do not move this airplane until I say to," I told him. We stayed dead level with the basket for at least a minute. I could hear his breathing continue to slow down. "OK, move up, start easing in. Stop."

I called Stabilized to Basketball and got the cleared-to-plug return call. We inched toward the basket nicely at 230 knots airspeed. That was tanking.

"It's at your one o'clock, Joker, eighteen inches," I said. "We are going to do this now, *Now*. Make your play. Smoothly, Joker, smoothly." He lanced the probe in, sighed, and we got the green-light call from Basketball. Fuel was flowing. We stayed plugged in, took our fuel, disengaged and were free to continue on to the target. Both of us were breathing easier.

He had been honest about all of it. He *was* a good bomber. We did our job and recovered in the Garden. He waited until all the other crew had left before walking up to me. He grabbed my left bicep in his big ham fist and looked me straight in the eye. "Thanks," was all he said.

***

More than a year later, I was in Austin, Texas, working as an officer selection officer, OSO, recruiting officers for the Marines. Our office was small but our infantry captain wanted us to hold our own Marine Corps Birthday Ball.

In the peacetime Marine Corps, a Birthday Ball is a formal affair. A big deal. I was charged with finding an honored guest speaker, a senior. I thought about it for a minute.

"I might have someone. He sort of owes me," I told my grunt boss.

I tracked down Joker. He was out in Beaufort, South Carolina, at the time. The CO of MCAS Beaufort. He couldn't make the Ball because of a scheduling conflict but he was honored that I had thought of him. While on the phone he asked, "Do you need me to tell your boss about you and me? You need backup? You know I can tell him stories that'll make you a water-walker in his eyes, Fleet."

"No sir," I said. "He's a damned good man and will understand. Besides that, he would get twisted up if you did come. He was wondering that a lieutenant could call up a bird colonel and jaw with him informally. You know how the grunts are."

Chapter 20. One Wild Ride

I then whispered to Joker that my captain was walking towards my door. I raised my voice slightly and asked, "So Joker, done any tanking lately?"

Joker laughed out loud. I held the phone away because he laughed so hard it hurt my ear. My captain could hear it too, looked puzzled and grinned. Joker became a minister after retiring from the Marine Corps. He passed away years back. When I became a bird colonel, I thought of him often and that wild-ass ride around the tanker. And about honesty. By then I was merely an old, not so bold, used-to-be fighter RIO.

Chapter 21

The Ten-Degree Run

February 1973

In February 1973, I logged 30.6 hours of flight time, 22.8 hours of that combat time, in 23 hops out of The Rose Garden spread over 23 days. Every RIO in VMFA-115 was flying his buns off. Seemed to me then and now, RIOs were in short supply. Other Silver Eagle RIOs had as much flight time that month, as many combat hops, as I did—or more. The operational tempo was high. Very. The Southeast Asia conflict we were in was still very much on.

***

One hop of that time stands out. My pilot was Beak. He was our aviation maintenance officer, a major, already a Heavy. Later he became a lieutenant general, three-star. Some pilots bore watching but according to the informal, back-channel RIOs Protective Association grapevine, Beak was good. He was one of those Heavies we instinctively respected. Respect and trust just went to men like him. And not because of the piece of shiny metal on their collars.

Though I was still a first lieutenant, I had already become a mission commander. I was salty enough to know that rank was not a deal-breaker in the plane, especially on a combat hop. Beak was simply my stick and I was his scope.

Flying with Beak, I wanted to bring my A-game. As we boarded the Phantom on a hot morning, I thought to myself, *Lord, help me not to screw this one up.* Beak and I reefed and zorched out of The Rose Garden as Section Lead. The heat made it harder to get airborne and we were doing whatever it took. Yanking and banking. Hard-core flying.

We aerial refueled per standard operating procedure. Beak was good on the tanker despite the fact that we had a full load of ordnance. We crossed the Mekong, then switched up to airborne command-and-control frequency, fire-checked chaff and flares, all without incident. We didn't

110

know exactly where we were headed other than to a route package of some number, one through six, which ACC told us and then handed us off to our FAC. When we checked in with the FAC, he would finally give us the mission, tell us what kind of target we would be taking on.

We were under the control of a Raven FAC on this hop. Based in Vientiane, Laos, the Ravens were, hands down, the best contingent of FACs we worked with. In their little propeller-driven airplanes, they were utterly fearless and deadly accurate. Their reputation was solid, theater-wide. They had suffered many lost planes and shot-down pilots. But they took the air war straight down on the enemy, regardless. Like them, we would get down low in the weeds to see, identify and destroy a target. Or at least try.

The FAC described our target as a possible track-mounted, heavy-caliber gun, 85-millimeter, hidden in a karst or cliff face. The bad guys had covered the entrance to the cave and camouflaged the rails the gun rode on with brush. The FAC thought he knew where the cave was but he was certain that lately this gun had been raising hell for our ground ops in the area. It had a 15-mile range and shot a projectile half the size of a Volkswagen Beetle. A deadly weapon.

To hit this target, we needed the precision that low-angle bombing would give us. We figured out quickly that this hop would be a ten-degree run. We would be flying almost flat at low altitude across a plain in a valley running perpendicular to the cliff. We would need all the speed we could get.

***

Low-angle attacks, like a 10-degree run, were a different ballgame from the 30-degree or 45-degree runs we usually flew. The big plus, the lower we flew, the better we could actually see the target. The big minus, flying low and flat was more dangerous. The bad guys could see us *and* low-angle bombing was less efficient. For the most efficient bombing, the plane flew at a steeper angle toward its target. Flying low, the plane flew slower and speed was life.

Earlier in the war, 1966–1970, in our stateside training we had used weapons such as nape and snake, which would have been useful in low-angle attacks. Napalm, jellied gasoline in a lightweight aluminum canister, was the best low-angle attack weapon when troops-in-contact were the target. Snake Eye bombs were 500-pounders that popped out four fan-like fins upon release. Their fins acted as a metal parachute and slowed the time of fall and impact of that weapon. Theoretically, the high drag resulting from the fins gave the bomber time to get out of his own frag pattern from a low-release altitude. Fragments of bombs that had just been dropped could rebound higher than the plane and blow up the bomber.

We had been trained stateside for a different war where the enemy mainly had World War II–vintage anti-aircraft artillery with optical sights. But by 1973, the Air Order of Battle had changed. The defenses we encountered as we attacked a target had changed. They were more accurate and sophisticated. Several were radar guided as opposed to optically sighted.

The presence of these more sophisticated weapons had pushed our minimum floor to around 4,000 feet, lower than the Air Force floor, which was around 6,000 feet. They were more concerned with SAM-7 and radar-guided ZSU-23 threats than the Marines were. We used what ordnance we had. We carried what were generically called slicks, Mark 82, 500-pound low-drag bombs that fell quickly. Still, we had to watch our P's and Q's so as not to frag ourselves. At times we carried daisy cutters, Mark 82s with a 36-inch fuse extender, a length of pipe screwed into the nose of the bomb. The bomb detonated three feet off the ground. The blast and frag went horizontally. We always had a Zuni pack of five-inch self-propelled rockets as forward-firing ordnance for flack suppression. Sometimes they were lethal. The idea was to keep the heads of the shooters down when they saw projectiles come at them off the airplane at roll-in. It helped spoil their aim.

The arsenal at The Rose Garden included other weapons such as the Rockeye that would have been effective in bombing the limestone cliff on the ten-degree hop. But we didn't have it on board the day of this hop. We hadn't known that we might need it because we hadn't known what we were going up against. In addition to its bombs, the F-4 also carried two air-to-air missiles, one Sparrow and one Sidewinder, plus two 370-gallon external wing tanks. All in all, the fully loaded F-4 B of the Silver Eagles was heavy. A graph in the Naval Aviation Training Operations Standardization manual, or NATOPS, showed that our fully loaded plane was on the edge of marginal controllability. But Beak could play that airplane like a piano.

***

This hop was one of those pilot-feel runs and the Beak was feeling pretty good. In the front cockpit, he set up the weapons-switch panel, called the dog bone because of its shape, and armed the bombs. He would have to draw on all his experience and intuition on this hop, recalculating the drop point in mid-run to compensate for the low altitude and low-drag ordnance.

Chapter 21. The Ten-Degree Run

We went over my mark call point and the rest of what we would do. I was to gape out of the quarter panels of my cockpit at the cliff we were running at and call where I thought the mark should be. We were low, very low, probably around 500 feet, trying for the speed of heat, every knot both afterburners could give. Speed was uppermost in my RIO brain. Speed was life.

The FAC had marked with a *willie pete*, then corrected, and called the impact point from there. Beak said he had it and in we went, cleared hot, okay to bomb. Because of the long run-in, I had time to look left and right. Damn, we were low. Small arms and SAM-7 low, but we were trucking, 500 knots and building, hauling it over bare earth toward the cliff. I called the speed. We were up to 520 knots but Beak said we weren't there yet. Peripherally, I could see that the cliff and our target enemy gun were coming up fast. Our angle was flatter than ten degrees. We were level. Beak said we were good.

We were in his hands until I couldn't stand it anymore and hollered, "Pickle Pull!" at exactly the moment when Beak dropped the first five bombs. The bombs looked like big pickles and as they fell, Beak pulled the plane up steeply. A lot of gravity, eight Gs to be precise, came on the bird. We were grunting in a valsalva maneuver, a hold-your-breath-and-push-out maneuver that gave us approximately half a G more tolerance as our bodies wanted to black out with blood being pulled out of our brains. I groaned, "Lead's off."

At our low altitude, I could feel the detonations of the first bombs as thumps. I turned in my seat and checked for SAM-7 corkscrew smoke trails headed for us, signaling enemy fire. None. We were going to make two passes at the target. Later, our group skipper Joker would change the Rules of Engagement, outlawing more than one pass at a target. Make one pass and come home. But on this day, multiple passes were still allowed.

As we climbed up, leveled off and banked left to reenter the race-track formation with our Wingman, the FAC was going nuts. "Son of a bitch!" he yelled. "Lead, you blew the doors off! They're pouring out like ants!"

"Two, hit Lead's smoke, cleared hot." The FAC gave our Wingman clearance to bomb and Two put his bombs right in the throat of the cave. The Raven was ecstatic, "Good hits, Two." Then to us, "Lead, cleared hot."

On our second run, we made the same approach but this time not from as far back and a bit slower. As the Thai would say, "Nit noi." Just a little slower. Beak had this one wired. Now the target was enemy troops in the open.

I know Beak strung out the second bomb load as best he could to do maximum damage, rather than dropping the bombs in one clump. I again yelled, "Pull!" as he started a climbing turn in full afterburner. We pulled up so hard we may have even overstressed the airplane. Beak mumbled something. He was an aviation maintenance officer after all.

While feeling the whumps, I looked over my left shoulder to see the hits. I saw dirty orange flame and dirt smoke. I also saw little dark stick figures cartwheeling through the air. The BDA came from our still excited FAC while we circled high and dry, *switches safe*: "BDA, 100 over 100, one heavy gun destroyed. Thirteen KBA." Killed by air. My first FAC-confirmed killed by air. Those little stick figures in the air.

We joined up with Two to check each other over for battle damage as we pointed the Phantoms toward Da Nang, where we would refuel, rearm, debrief, rebrief and then fly another hop on our way back to the Garden. Out of my 131 red-ink hops, this was my only ten-degree run, my first KBA. An 85-millimeter gun in a cliff on a low, flat hairy run. Good BDA and Beak and I both made it back.

CHAPTER 22

Angkor Wat/Ankle What

Late February 1973

We began to suspect the war was winding down. Orders down from the senior controlling agency for the entire air war gave us fewer and fewer sorties as we moved toward spring 1973.

Missions into Vietnam had stopped. Missions into Laos had stopped. That left us flying only into Cambodia and we really didn't know why. Aircrews didn't have much true intelligence as to the targets we were after. We sure as hell weren't given the big picture. The only Americans we knew about in Cambodia, if any Americans were there at all, were embassy people. The only specific Cambodian name kicked around was Pol Pot. Few of us knew much about him—then.

What we did know was if we were on the schedule, we flew the hop. Those hops into Cambodia were arduous and so long that they required two refuelings from the tanker, once going down and again coming back. For navigation, we had to rely on the primitive analog computer in the plane and dead-reckoning navigation. Plus we still had to contend with defensive gunfire over the targets.

In February 1973, my pilot Nacho and I were leading a Section down to Cambodia. Our Phantom had a standard load. On this hop, Nacho had asked me to take some pictures with his camera. The flight's route had us going over Angkor Wat, a famous and historic Hindu temple. I took Nacho's camera as we boarded old bureau number 152300, the F-4 B assigned to us. While we waited to launch, Nacho told me he would roll up on the plane's knife edge with wings perpendicular to the ground for a good picture over the temple. Fine.

Start, taxi, take off, all normal. We fenced with the tanker, refueled southeast of Nam Phong and were topped off. We would cross the Mekong and soon be in bad guy country. It was time to arm up the missiles, chaff and flares. Angkor Wat was about fifteen minutes ahead.

I kept up minimal navigational commentary for Nacho so he could spot the temple out front. We flew in combat spread, which put our Wingman half a mile off to the side, flying, as we were, straight and level. Nacho and I didn't want the other plane to know what we were up to with the picture. If that crew thought something was amiss when Nacho turned the plane on its wing edge, we'd just tell them to disregard it.

We had little idea of what the actual combat mission would be. We would find out soon enough after check-in with the FAC down the line. We knew we'd find the FAC's little prop plane slowly droning around below us looking for suspected enemy concentrations.

But before getting to the FAC, we were concerned with getting the picture of what Pennsylvania hillbilly Nacho called Ankle What.

"There it is," Nacho said from the front. "Get the camera ready." I switched on Nacho's camera, took off the lens cap and plastered my eye to the eyepiece. His Canon was different from my Minolta but I figured the cameras were enough alike that I should be able to get him the pictures he wanted.

Nacho quarter-rolled the airplane up, still holding the nose level. I told the Wingman to disregard the wing flash as I saw the triangular temple below and snapped the shutter.

Nothing clicked. The shutter was frozen. When Nacho asked me if I got the picture, I told him what happened. "No sweat," he said. "We'll get it on the return leg." I squared the camera away and stowed it.

We went back to wings level and pressed on to the Tonle Sap, a huge lake that was impossible to miss and therefore was a waypoint in Cambodia. We checked in with the FAC, got our mission and hit the target, an ammo dump as I recall. We took fire. After we hit the target, I updated the navigation computer for the return trip. Angkor Wat was about five minutes away. Our Wingman figured out what we were up to and stayed quiet as we approached the triangular temple.

"OK," Nacho said and once again took the plane over on the knife edge. I focused on the triangle below and snapped the picture. As I looked, I could see shiny specks between us and the ground.

"Nach," I said, "we're taking fire." He swore, flipped level, put the nose thirty degrees up, lit the afterburners and got us out of gun range. It was problem enough to get hit in a run over a hot target. It was unacceptable to get hit on a photo opportunity, no matter how old or sacred the temple. It doesn't take a lot of fire to knock a plane down but that day we were safe. We flew back to The Rose Garden feeling seriously chastened.

The picture of the temple turned out well and Nacho made copies of

116

the snapshot for me. Neither of us would have forgotten that run anyway but the picture makes it doubly memorable. We could clearly see the glints of light as the camera caught the rounds coming towards us.

CHAPTER 23

Drop the Hook

March 1973

First, I have to parse my Dogs. The original Dog was landlord of the infamous Doghouse hootch next door to Maggotville, where I lived with the various Maggots. Dog was one hell of a soul besides being an accomplished stick.

Underscoring Dog's skill and finesse in the bird, he went from The Rose Garden to maybe the most coveted assignment a Marine aviator can get, The Blue Angels, the Navy's flight demonstration team. That assignment brought with it rock-star status among Marines because the U.S. Navy used only one Marine pilot per Blue Angels team. The plane flown by the Marine pilot is always number two in tail number and in the flight formation.

But the Dog I am thinking of just now had the callsign Maddog. After the original Dog rotated out, however, Maddog became plain old Dog, just to keep things interesting. One afternoon during a lull, Maddog and I were doing a post-maintenance check flight on a bird just out of heavy work. Northwest of Nam Phong we were to twirl the bird around and make sure what had been repaired worked as advertised. We had lots of gas and a clean airplane. Only bomb racks and missile rails, no ordnance. Off we went.

Coming up on the appropriate frequencies, we started putting the bird through its paces. Everything worked. Halfway through the test flight, though, a transmission came from a control agency, ordering us to take up a certain heading, arm our weapons and go into full afterburner. We had been told to take a vector to an actual air-to-air threat, a MiG.

I responded, "Roger, Out." Maddog yanked the plane onto the heading and called, "Roger, Armstrong." He had indicated that our missiles were armed. A lie, but one that would allow us to pursue a MiG.

My heart went into afterburner and my eyes went down to the radar. We were in a run, committed. I rogered the call and put the radar in 50-mile scale. I was looking hard at the scope. As we came to the heading, I reminded him that we were out of ordnance. "Dog, we're Winchester. This is a test hop."

Chapter 23. Drop the Hook

But he cut me short. "No problem," he said. "We'll just lower the tail-hook and rip the bastard." And on we roared. In for a penny, in for a pound. But further down the run at 11 miles from the target, we got a knock-it-off call from the agency. Stop the attack, slow up, go back to what we were doing. We did just that, wondering what in the hell had just gone down.

Back in the Garden, we learned that a man standing in the jump door of a C-130 going south down the Mekong River had seen a flash zip by and thought it was a MiG. That became the vector. Some MiGs were painted silver. The man had seen the silver flash and drawn the wrong conclusion. False alarm.

A decade or so later, I was sitting in the O-Club at MCAS Yuma, while our unit was deployed there. I was having a cocktail after a hop. A RIO I did not know walked up, looked at my name tag and said, "You were with Maddog the day you guys got a vector and Maddog was gonna lower the tailhook and rip the bastard!"

I had no idea how that story had made it out into the sea-story mill that is part of the lore of Marine fighter aviation. Must have been a slow news day. "Yeah," I told him, and he bought me a drink.

***

Maddog's aggressive plan was not without precedent. In World War II, at least one Marine aviator had wound up in a furball of Japanese planes. The Marine was out of ammunition. In the spirit of the battle, he lowered his tailhook, whose real purpose was to arrest a plane in a shipboard landing. He opted to fly close above and perpendicular to the rudder of the enemy airplane. He tore off the rudder and sent the enemy into the ocean.

***

I had been taken aback, to put it mildly, by this hop with Maddog. But had the knock-it-off call not come, I know we would have pressed. Maddog would have tried to rip the bastard. Maybe he could have pulled it off.

CHAPTER 24

Upside Down
and Embarrassed

March 1973

During a lull in combat hops, Beak and I went out on a maintenance hop to check that the work previously done on the bird had really fixed what had been wrong. We flew in the local area because it was not a combat hop. We were not loaded with anything except the bomb racks and Sidewinder missile rails.

We began our maintenance check work around 25 miles or so east of The Rose Garden and did not go to high altitude, just high enough to do loops and rolls and check out the flight controls.

When we took off, I thought this hop would be a piece of cake. Both Beak and I had done numerous test hops previously and they were no big deal. We were far enough from The Rose Garden that the plane's tactical aid to navigation, or TACAN, our main means of finding the air field, unlocked. My TACAN needle began spinning, receiving no signal. The TACAN was reliable most of the time but because the TACAN unit at The Rose Garden was an expeditionary model with limited range and reliability, it would go down in rainy weather or if the aircraft was too far away from the field. Or maybe all our test gyrations had caused it to unlock.

As Beak put the bird through its paces, doing several loops and rolls and dives, I realized I was having the onset of vertigo. Not wanting to tell Beak out of misplaced pride, I said nothing until we got ready to return to The Rose Garden.

Then I had to admit to Beak I was all fouled up, AFU, and couldn't tell where we were. *And* the TACAN wasn't working. I put my head down as close to my knees as I could for a minute to let my head clear, then raised up, trying to create a horizon. I was partially successful. Beak got us back to The Rose Garden without incident because he had stayed situationally aware, knew roughly where we had flown and had a working compass.

Chapter 24. Upside Down and Embarrassed

I started apologizing from the back seat but he was OK. It was a good thing we had never left Thailand, the weather was clear more than not, and nobody was shooting at us. I knew I was exhausted. Leading up to that hop, I had been flying almost daily. All RIOs had been. Maybe that explained the vertigo. But I never expected this kind of situation to show up on a plain vanilla hop. The usual adrenaline kick from a combat hop had just never shown up on this test hop.

We got back and were writing up the bird's performance, debriefing as it were. I expected some heat and steam, or at least hard kidding—all of which I deserved—from the Beak but it never came because of the understanding officer, pilot, and man he consistently was.

To this day, and my memory is especially clear here, this hop is the most embarrassing one I flew from The Rose Garden. To make it worse, I had been in the backseat of the last pilot I would have wanted this experience to happen with. I had been a seasoned RIO one day and felt like a little mousy vertigoed-out guy the next. I was the once-caricatured RIO who was little more than 160-pounds of ballast.

When I think of humbling experiences in my life, this hop is near the top of them.

Special Times, Special People

CHAPTER 25

Gracie L. Zoobreath

November 1972

Sometimes callsigns were both capriciously given and changeable. One of the more colorful callsigns in the Silver Eagles was Gracie L. Zoobreath. His first callsign was Filthy but we decided that was unacceptable *and* we just wanted to mess with him. Someone changed his callsign to Gracie L. Zoobreath but he was just Gracie or maybe Zoobreath in the air.

In actual life, he was a senior captain, a second or third tour pilot, a proven stick. He was not harsh with me as I broke in during my early days. He was a good guy. It was impossible not to like Gracie.

When flying in Gracie's backseat, I heard the friendly, but illegal, call-and-response system, that Gracie and his RIO buddy had worked out just to keep up with each other. The two men had been in the same squadron on their first or second tours in Vietnam. Knew each other well. Flying in different planes, one of them would come up on Guard frequency, which was to be used only during emergencies, and say, "Mach-mach." The other would respond, "Nit noi." Those were Thai words for much-much and a teeny bit. I never knew what was behind this gambit. I never asked. I just laughed.

Gracie was the main attraction at one of our All Officers Meetings. In most of the AOMs, Clipper would pass the word on what we were doing, which of the six route packages we might expect to go to. Brief hail-and-farewells were held for those FNGs arriving or the lucky salts returning to the world. At the end, Skipper would open the floor to general conversation.

At one of those meetings, we learned about Gracie's upcoming farewell. Not a normal rotation. He had been diagnosed by one of the two flight surgeons in Nam Phong with elephantiasis, a swelling from accumulation of fluid which had located in one of his testicles. The condition was extremely uncomfortable and he was put in a down or no-fly status because he could not fit into his flight suit. Treating the problem was beyond the capability of our dispensary, which was far below what television's well-loved "M*A*S*H" could do. Our docs decided to medevac him to Yokosuka, Japan, for treatment and repair.

As Clipper announced that Gracie would be leaving, he stood up, covered in skivvies, but still with an obvious swelling. The size of a tennis ball. He said, "Skipper, I now have a career after the Marine Corps. I can be a freak in a Tijuana side-show." That killed everybody. The laughing went on for five minutes. But we also knew that Gracie showed a certain amount of grace in dealing with a tough situation.

Gracie was discharged from the hospital but by then time was too short for him to re-train and re-enter the squadron at The Rose Garden. Clipper had gotten a quota to fill for an experienced Aircraft Maintenance Officer, the officer in charge of the Naval Aviation Engineering Service Unit outfit in Cubi Point. It was a plum job but with heavy responsibility. Under normal circumstances in the Navy or Marine Corps, this position would require a rank of major or higher but field grade officers were in short supply during the war and senior captains, like Gracie, were often elevated for such positions.

The best part was it got Gracie out of Nam Phong. He lived in a real building, with a real bed, air conditioning, running water, constant electricity, and good meals prepared by Navy mess men.

Once we knew where Gracie had gone, we made it a habit when we flew a bird over to Cubi and waited for a new one to fly back, to make what became a famous page. We would go to the Navy Yeoman in the Cubi Officers Club and ask him to page Captain Zoobreath, Captain Gracie L. Zoobreath.

We always got a bang out of it. And Gracie knew when we were in town.

CHAPTER 26

Me and Mr. Tones

December 1972

From time to time, Clipper doled out trips to desirable places. Anywhere outside of The Rose Garden. Because the war was theoretically winding down by the time I arrived in the Garden, there was no more traditional R&R. The best we could do was go on a business trip for the squadron. We would have what might be called *amenities* as well as a chance with a very small number of American women. Usually the school teachers on base.

The trips didn't come free. Part of a business trip was, well, squadron business. Clipper might ask us to take or pick up a bird at Atsugi, Japan, ferry a bird across for a missile shoot or take a bird that had the requisite hours of flying over for inspection of its engines, systems and airframe. The planes were flown hard and needed regular checks.

It was on such a check-cycle flight that my friend Tones and I took an airplane from The Rose Garden across to Cubi Point. I liked Tones. He was from Plaquemines Parrish, Louisiana. Shorter than most of us, compactly built and almost wiry, Tones was a superb athlete and usually had a grin on his mug. He had a last name that suggested he might be of Russian descent and we'd hardly expect any Cajun-ness from him. But it was there. He could veer off into that unique patois with little prompting. Because he was a joyful and lively man known to break out into a popular song with no warning, he was just the right kind of buddy to go with on a half-assed R&R business trip. Our operations officer told us the check crew at Cubi was expecting us.

The check-and-repair cycle took a while, too long for us to wait, so on these runs we were expected to fly right back in another bird that was up and running. That was the rule but we would usually be able to milk one or two additional days out of the trip by telling our ops guys in the Garden that the next plane was almost ready. But not quite.

When I saw that we were on the flight schedule for the hop, I walked over to Tones' hootch to tell him. "Tones," I said, sticking my head in, "we're on for Cubi. Get yourself together, lad!"

He was still asleep since it was his day off. He rolled over in his rack and wiped the jungle muck out of his eyes, yawned widely and said, "Well, fuck me to tears, Grittus. When do we launch?"

"Eleven hundred," I answered in military time. "We're taking the Eight Ball."

Number Zero Eight was a bird with a reputation for screwy technical problems. I had flown a strange bombing hop in it weeks before. During a 45-degree dive, it felt as if we were sitting atop a ball swivel like the one a desk-set ballpoint pen balances on. The swiveling had been disconcerting to both me and the pilot. After that flight, we downed the plane. It had been fixed since then. Theoretically. Its appearance was as odd as its behavior. The bird was unmistakable. It had a solid black nose while the other Silver Eagle birds had white noses. Thus, it became the Eight Ball for its number, appearance and reputation. I was a tad on guard about flying the Eight Ball because it had weirded out on me already. But not Tones. Our maintenance men were good. If the schedule said a bird was up, it was up.

"Who gives a damn?" Tones asked. "Cubi? I'd fly a paper airplane to get to Cubi."

"Bullshit," I responded. "You'd rather have a pirogue or a bateau. Maybe trap a few nutria along the way. Snag a gator."

Tones laughed and then shifted the subject. "You got your baht gun loaded?" he asked, wanting to know if I had money.

"Damn right I do but we'll be shooting Philippine pesos today, extra clips sewn on to the zoom bag." I was loaded.

"We're gonna be somebody, Grittus, my man!" said Tones, finally awake and enthusiastic. I agreed. We were ready for whatever Cubi Point offered.

***

At 11:00 a.m., Tones and I launched out of the Garden and headed almost due east for the Philippine Islands, the P.I. Except for the external fuel tanks, the bird was considered clean—no bombs, no missiles, no rockets. Clean or not, the plane needed a steady eye on its fuel gauge. We got as much altitude as we could as fast as we could to save fuel. Tones and I kept a close eye on how much gas we had burned.

Flying east, we reminded ourselves that our main and last visual checkpoint would be directly overhead Da Nang. If we were overhead Da Nang with enough gas and on the correct heading, we would be good to go at least to the go/no-go point we had plotted ahead of time.

Our go/no-go point was a navigational fix plotted out in the South

China Sea. It was just a mark on a map but it was an important one. It indicated the point by which we had to turn around if something was amiss because we wanted to have enough gas to make it back to Da Nang. Generally, there was no reason to turn around unless something happened well before that point.

From 31,000 feet, the long parallel runways of Da Nang were little pencil marks that ran north towards the mountains. The runways and the coastal location on Half Moon Bay made Da Nang a landmark that was hard to miss from any altitude. During that last year of war, Da Nang was the busiest airport in the world. The fuel issue mandated that we be directly over it and damned sure we were on heading.

***

During any flight from Da Nang to the Philippine Islands, a RIO would remember the story of Prince Otto the Navigator, the RIO on a bird that almost completely missed the Philippine Islands a few years back. When the crew on that bird finally figured out their mistake, they flew towards what they thought was the mainland but what they found was only deserted beach a hundred miles south of Cubi Point. Within minutes of their discovery, they had lined up the airplane with the beach and shit-canned the Phantom.

That event and what happened to the crew when they got back to base became a legend. All of Marine Corps F-4 fighter aviation knew this crew had *missed* the Philippine Islands. Their screw-up loomed large and not in a good way.

***

Although Tones and I were primed to rest and recreate, we kept our wits about us while en route. We made it to Da Nang with ample fuel. There was no need yet to transfer fuel from the external wing tanks into the feed cell on top of the engines. We were on heading—fat, dumb and happy. We had enough fuel, were alone and were headed for Cubi with money.

Tones was feeling good enough that he broke out into a popular Seals & Crofts song of the time, "Summer Breeze." He was fond of making up his own words to the popular songs we all knew. For this one he corrupted the original lyrics by injecting his own. *That gust of wind makes me feel fine, 'specially when I'm parked on Cubi's l-iiiii-ne.* Tones had a voice that could hit a strong rock-and-roll falsetto easily with no shame.

I told him that if it took his own sorry off-key-assed singing to stay

129

heads-up, then he could sing away. He muttered a foul obscenity in Cajun. Even feeling good, we stayed focused. The fuel transfer was not automatic, never a sure bet. It required switch changes and an ability to calculate quickly. If something went wrong, the fuel could become trapped and trapped fuel meant unusable fuel, which was nothing more than excess weight. Which, if you have to get somewhere, is actual, real drag.

Although Tones was a rank higher than I was—a captain—he had less time in-country than I had, so practically speaking he was junior to me. Like a lot of guys who arrived green, his start at the Garden had been inglorious but by the time we made our trip to Cubi, he was solid, could hit a target and knew the *switchology* required to get the fuel transferred out of the external tanks. He did it routinely.

He started getting ready to transfer fuel when we were just short of our go/no-go point out over the South China Sea.

"No need to worry till we get there," I said to Tones with false bravado I was soon to regret. Before a later airframe change, there were no fuel gauges in the rear cockpit. The RIO had to ask, to bug the pilot about fuel status.

Only a minute later, I heard a concerned Tones speak a strong, "Shit!" through the earphones on my helmet. "We're almost to the go/no-go and the fucking fuel is not transferring!" he said. "It's trapped." The fuel gauge showed him what was happening, or not happening in this case.

As we considered our options, Tones continued to watch the gauge indicating that fuel transfer from the wing tanks had stopped altogether, if it ever had really started. We pulled out the emergency checklists we all carried. I turned to the section on no fuel transfer from external tanks. As the clock ticked away and we got farther and farther out to sea, we tried every switch position listed on the checklist with no positive results.

We were so focused on these different attempts that we had flown right through the go/no-go point. We were several miles beyond it before I figured out what we'd done. By the time I fixed our position and looked at where we were, we had two choices. Get the fuel to transfer or ditch, put the plane in the water and take our chances with sharks. If we survived the sharks, we would then be looking at facing long-term humiliation. Somehow, we had to get the fuel going out of the external tanks and into the engines. Or swim.

We nosed up to a higher altitude to allow the engines to run on less gas. We were both quiet, both thinking and both pushing away thoughts of having to go swimming. As I told myself to think and think hard, I remembered a wild-card tip the great older F-4 RIO, the He Coon, had given me back at Cherry Point just before a test-and-acceptance hop. He Coon had seen everything go wonky with an F-4 that could go wrong. As He Coon and I walked to the bird for that test hop, he had told me, *if you're getting no fuel transfer at all from the external tanks, go to full hot on the cabin air conditioner.*

Though every plane was supposedly air-conditioned, the system seldom worked as advertised. That was the reason for the chamois skins we all carried. They allowed us to mop up the sweat and still see. It was a tidbit that hadn't made sense to me at the time but I had never had a reason to test it. Now with no other options I figured we had to try.

Over the South China Sea, I thought about He Coon's advice. Knowing there was no technical reason for a trick like that to work, I still hoped like hell that it would. I told Tones the crazy procedure the older RIO had suggested and without a word he reset the switches.

We were already sweating like young pigs. Fear sweat. Instantly the bird got hot inside. Heat and sweat were draining our energy and increasing our anxiety level—not a good combination. As the hot air poured into the plane, the gauges began to show the usable fuel within the fuselage tanks was building. Transfer was happening.

***

We had a chance now. We were about two-thirds of the way to the Philippines, feeling a little better even if soaked and stinking. But before relief could fully settle in, the second Eight Ball gotcha happened.

We had almost passed the mandatory check-in point, a place on the map called the Air Defense Identification Zone, or ADIZ. At this point, aircraft were required to tell the local government they were about to enter its sovereign airspace. Like our go/no-go point, the ADIZ entry point was out over the water. In the scrambling to avoid fuel starvation, I had let the ADIZ sneak up on me. It was a big no-no to enter another nation's airspace without clearance. It created an international incident.

Generally, when a nation realized its air space was possibly being violated without proper notice, it assumed the aircraft was manned by hostile intruders. The subject nation had the right—and frequently exercised that right—to scramble armed interceptor aircraft with the understanding that such aircraft might be ordered to shoot the invading plane down.

The U.S. does it all the time. I had intercepted such planes several times when I was stateside. Each time instead of hostile intruders, I found only lost, dazed or confused aviators. Most often civilians.

Realizing the position we were in, I quickly switched the radio frequency to Guard, a clear-channel frequency used only for emergencies. I sent out a message to Stargazer, a ship that acted as ADIZ Control, giving our position, which I fudged to legality, and our revised ETA. I waited. No response. Shit. I sent out the message again and waited as we pressed on.

After a long few minutes, I got a weak, scratchy reply. "Duckbutt here, over," a voice said from an amphibious Coast Guard airplane monitoring the Guard frequency. Duckbutt was on patrol to pick up unfortunates who had ditched. I told the radio operator that we were unable to raise Stargazer and asked him to pass along to Stargazer and the Philippine authorities ASAP our transmission of a revised ETA and penetration of Philippine airspace. "Roger," he said.

Tones and I looked at each other in the mirrors and breathed sighs of relief. Another bullet dodged. We were dry and legal after all. By now though we were no longer fat, dumb and happy but lean, watchful and concerned. We'd had a close call and we weren't exactly home free.

***

Tones and I talked about our options. We considered doing a straight-in approach at Cubi Point to save fuel but that would not have looked good around the air patch and looking good was important. So we opted for a showier and more proper way for a fighter to enter the air patch. Approaching the landing strip at Cubi, I asked Tones to check the gauges one last time. The fuel-level low-light was on bright and steady.

We did a snappy break, descended, lowered the gear, got clearance and made an uneventful landing. We congratulated ourselves silently while we taxied towards the visiting aircraft line.

No sooner had I switched up Ground Control frequency for taxi approval, than a deep voice came over the radio, "Blade 08, upon shutdown report to Base Ops. Out." Somehow the shit had hit the fan. We were never told to go to Base Ops unless something was wrong.

Since Cubi was a U.S. Naval Base, the command we had received meant that Tones and I would shortly be standing before a senior sailor, a Naval officer. We would have to stand at attention with our heels locked, explaining ourselves or, worse, being made to defend and perhaps cover up something we had done wrong. We got out of the plane slowly, took off our flight gear and put on our soft covers, trying to delay the ass-chewing that was headed our way. Like many good fighter pukes, we decided to go with the cover-up option so we started to get our stories straight.

Tones asked, "Grittus, you tape that hop?"

Chapter 26. Me and Mr. Tones

"Damned sure did," I told him. He smiled that old Mr. Tones smile. All RIOs carried small tape recorders so the debriefers and other guys could listen and learn what had been done right or wrong.

He stopped. "Play it," he said, still smiling. "I want to hear it once before we get shot. But then erase all the bad stuff and leave in the good stuff."

I knew what was on it—the good, the bad, and the ugly. I had already edited some of tape while we were in the airplane, knowing what was coming. I saved the pieces with Stargazer and Duckbutt, times adjusted to protect the guilty. Just in case. We rehearsed our story, put on our best mock-contrite Marine officer faces and walked toward the big building with the rotating beacon on top. Base Ops.

Along the way, not having a choice on what was about to happen to us, we laughed at the prospects. We said things to each other like *What are they gonna do to us? Shave our heads and send us to Vietnam? Make us go live in tents for a year and become best buds with the Nam Phong screamers?* Brave but hollow talk. We both knew there was a real possibility the words *international incident* could be in our futures. And records.

We didn't fool ourselves that we might be shown mercy. We had been the so-called hand of justice in other military proceedings. More than once I had been a part of proceedings where someone said *bring the guilty bastards in.* Tones was the squadron legal officer for VMFA-115. He knew the Uniform Code of Military Justice.

Worse than the threat of an international incident was the possibility that we could lose our wings. We would embarrass ourselves, our outfit, our skipper, our friends and the Marine Corps. Alone or in combination these possible consequences made up the worst-case scenario. And at the very least, a bad outcome could ruin our chance for rest and relaxation. It was all hard to take when we had just been so damned heroic. At least to ourselves.

The senior sailor turned out to be a Navy captain, J.S.T. Ragman, according to the brass plate on his door. The Navy equivalent of a Marine bird colonel, he was The Man. We stood outside Ragman's hatchway and pounded on it three times per Navy protocol, saying loudly that we were reporting as ordered. Sir. From inside, we heard his chair scrape back as he stood up. We then heard him clearly call out, "Enter."

The first thing I took in as I opened the door was that Ragman had that loaded-for-bear look, complete with scowl. He was wearing a white Alpha uniform that fit too tightly. His large belly hung over a tarnished belt buckle. Obviously, he did not suffer from missed-meal cramps. His face was red and he looked slightly apoplectic.

Section Three—Special Times, Special People

His office felt odd, incongruently homey. There was a floor lamp right out of Sears and Roebuck behind him rather than the typical fluorescent desk lamp. On the walls were plaques, mementoes and pictures of the Missus and kids. From his office we could tell that he had flown patrol aircraft, not fighters or attack planes. Although his office held many of the creature comforts I missed, I found no comfort in it.

We marched in uncovered, halted exactly, did a right face to his desk and stayed standing at rigid attention. We were good at that. We both had plenty of experience with ass-chewings by then. Ragman sat down and looked at his paperwork. He left us standing at attention, waiting as he looked over his papers. Finally, he put us at ease and after a long pause started in with a tense, "Gentlemen."

The Captain explained in a cold, flat voice that we had penetrated Philippine airspace without approval. He went on to say that we had come into that airspace at the wrong place, wrong altitude and off scheduled time. In response, the Philippine Air Defense Command had launched two F-5 fighters to intercept us and investigate.

"Gentlemen, thanks to you there are some pissed-off, highly placed Filipinos," he said, leaning back in his chair, pot belly protruding even farther. "What do you have to say about that?"

Since Tones was senior in rank, he spoke for us both. He explained we had struggled with trapped fuel almost the whole way after the go/no-go point and as a result had a lot of other things going on that took our attention. But, he said, we had reported to Stargazer, on time, on altitude and on course, via a relay that Duckbutt said he would make. The implication, of course, was this screw-up was Duckbutt's, not ours.

Without prompting I played the tape for the senior sailor three times. To make damned sure he heard it. He heard the attempt to contact Stargazer and the times in Zulu with no response, then the Duckbutt message. Tones explained that we were just going by what was on the tape. We had flown on while Stargazer, then Duckbutt stumbled. Our fix for the penetration of Philippine airspace, adjusted to make it appear legal, had been broadcast on Guard and was on tape.

To complicate matters, the Duckbutt squadron was stationed at Cubi Point and belonged to Ragman, who was CO of the Naval Air Station there. The Captain rolled his bulging eyes upward when he heard the sailor on Duckbutt give a Roger to our request. "Duckbutt strikes again," he said. "Fucking Coast Guard."

Strong language even for a sailor but the good news was that it wasn't aimed at us. Ragman was considering his own situation. At best, more paperwork for him. At worst, a budding international incident, which he alone would have to report somewhere. Upwards to his boss, an Admiral. We became bold in the face of his distress and knowing the best defense is a good offense, I asked, "Sir, why didn't we see the F-5s? If we'd seen them, we would've damn sure complied." I went on, "We'd have to be idiots not to. We were Winchester and hurting for gas," explaining that we carried no ammunition.

"The F-5s got lost," he said. "They almost ran out of fucking gas themselves."

Tones and I stood there for a full minute, waiting, wanting to smile but knowing better. Finally, the Captain looked up. It seemed that he had forgotten we were still there. He was already writing his report in his head.

"We may require you two to stay aboard a few more days to get this thing sorted out. We'll let you know. Dismissed," he said in a resigned voice. We took our requisite one step backward, halted, did a right face and marched smartly out of his office. Grinning at each other and thinking *oh, yeah, make us stay.*

***

Once out on the tarmac walking away from the building, Tones put his arm around my shoulder and said, "Good work, Grittus! Fuck these squid non-combatants. I'll have to remember that one. Trapped fuel in the externals? Go full-hot on the air conditioner. I nod to the He Coon."

I said, "Hey man, we got here and that's what counts. Not gonna have an international incident ruin our whole day."

"To the club, my man! We owe each other many drinks. The toast for today will be *fuck the squids*. All but the tailhookers." We did disparage the Navy but not our fellow combat fliers, the tailhookers. The flying Navy men landed with a tailhook on an aircraft carrier at sea, on a pitching deck at night, after combat. That commands respect from every other flyer then and now.

It was a good night for Tones and me. We drank enough to forget how bad we smelled and we had the best feeling a Marine pilot or RIO could have. Good Luck.

***

Some twenty years later, my friend Tones perished at sea in an AV-8 Harrier. The Harrier is a single seat airplane, pilot only. He had no RIO with

him. I find myself remembering him often and one of those times I wrote
this—

> *Tones never took a step that wasn't a spring.*
> *He sang often, and well he could sing.*
> *He was the best bridge player I ever knew.*
> *And I was the worst bridge player, too.*
> *So we did bridge partner-ing.*

Certain older songs, when I hear them now, still bring Tones, straight
and standing up, to my mind. When he would sing Billy Paul's "Me and Mrs.
Jones," another song popular from that time, Tones would make up his own
lyrics—

> *We meet every day ... in the usual way ... sixteen thirty...*

Semper Fidelis, Mr. Tones, friend of my youth. Friend now.

CHAPTER 27

Clipper Wins

December 1972

On an everyday basis, lieutenants and captains remained apart from senior officers, the Heavies, unless they had actual business or were on the same hop. They had responsibilities that we did not have. Senior officers made big decisions and ran the squadron. We held them in awe. Until we flew with them. Then it was callsigns and aircrew.

Most of the time, they kept their own counsel and could say and do things off-limits to junior officers. We thought there was a wide gulf separating us from them. It wasn't until later, when I became a Heavy myself, that I learned they were no different from anyone else. The reality was that the Heavies were simply older and more experienced. They were expected to know what to do and to do more. Most of our Heavies were on at least their second tour of duty in Vietnam. Clipper and Beak were on their third tours.

Because we saw them as being above us, it was always a revelation to watch the Heavies raise hell—the same kind of drunken hell that we raised. Often, their hell-raising had more color than ours since they had more money to spend and hell-raising was often connected to money—money spent, money owed. It wasn't unusual for Heavies to owe each other a lot of gambling money from ongoing craps and poker games. It also wasn't unusual for a major and a lieutenant colonel to come close to a fistfight over a hazy point of honor. As a rule, other Heavies would be placing their bets on a winner before the fight was even close to getting started.

***

In December 1972, when things were running hot and heavy flight-wise, Clipper was about halfway through his third tour. He was used to the privations of The Rose Garden and like the rest of us had grown to hate the place more every day. But he kept a good face on it.

One night we were in the Officers Club. As usual, three aircraft squadrons, our ground types and the infantry officers were all in attendance. We had also invited The Ravens down from Vientiane as our Rose Garden Happy Hour guests. We taught them the infamous Hooray cheer, one that a Silver Eagle had cooked up. The cheer was simple and inexplicable, done as a call and response:

> CALL: Can I get a WHO-RAY?
> RESPONSE: WHO-RAY, WHO-RAY, WHO-RAY!! EAGLES! ... PISS!

So popular was the cheer that we used it to decorate the inside of our airplanes' two-by-two-foot-wide red-panel bucket doors that popped open from both sides of the fuselage of the Phantom when we fired chaff bundles and flares. When flying next to an Air Force bird, we would give them a wink, opening these doors quickly to show the word *Hooray* stenciled in white inside the door. Air Force and Army flyers were very proper and didn't do that sort of thing.

Clipper was understanding of his men partying hard but it wasn't often that we saw him doing so. With The Ravens there, Clipper knew we would make a show of force at Happy Hour. By the time I got there, six jeeps were parked in a semi-circle out front of the palm-thatched roof that was our O-Club. The number of jeeps was impressive. Only squadron COs and up had jeeps. Having one was a big deal.

Also in attendance that night were guys from our Marine Airbase Squadron, MABS. We called them MABSters. Part of the support apparatus for a Marine Aircraft Group, the MABsters were a separate squadron with their own complement of officers and enlisted men. They worked for the same colonel we did, although somewhat lower down the totem pole of priority since we did the war-fighting. The CO and XO of the MABSters were pilots who flew when they could find hops to fly. The remainder of their officers were ground types who did not fly.

MABS was responsible for the runway, the crash crew, the fuel farm, the cherry picker and explosive ordnance disposal, among other things. If a plane ran off the runway into the dirt, their cherry-picker came and lifted it out. When bombs didn't come off the airplane, MABSters removed them, carried them away and then blew them up safely. The MABSters also owned all the jeeps and were responsible for them. They tended to be finicky about them and would not lend them out to just anyone.

Maybe jealousy over the jeeps was where the night's issues began. Or maybe it that the MABSters had just gotten a young major as their new CO and the old sorts were going to mess with him. Something.

***

Chapter 27. Clipper Wins

It wasn't meteorology that caused the low ceiling that night. Practically all hands were shitfaced except those that had an *early-early* the next day and the poor sap who was the group duty officer that night. The Silver Eagles were getting to know some of the Ravens we hadn't met. A better than good time was being had by all. Near midnight we began filtering out, weaving our way on foot back to the hootch area. The Ravens had been ensconced in the Visiting Officer Quarters, such as they were. In reality, the VOQ was just another set of hootches with cots and rubber ladies. I was hurting from the drinking so I went to my hootch and flopped down onto my rack. I was sawing wood in no time.

In less than an hour, all of us were unceremoniously awakened by a loud crash. In my booze-infused sleep, I was unsure what had happened. Might have been rounds fired at someone trying to get through the wire. As I sat up on my cot, I heard it again and recognized it—the unmistakable sound of one jeep crashing into another.

This was quickly followed by the sound of two jeep engines being thrown into reverse, engines revving, and then the unmistakable sound of metal smashing metal again. It didn't take me long to piece together that outside two men were engaged in a jeep duel. A weird high noon at midnight with jeeps. The next crash had a sense of loud finality. One engine sputtered, stalled and finally fell into silence. The other jeep engine continued coughing but running. The gears shifted and the sound of the second engine was drowned out by raucous laughing and swearing.

I heard a maniacal cackle followed by a command, a threat and a demand. "Wake up, buttheads! Come have a drink with your CO! You buncha assholes!" Then I heard the jeep roar and backfire with a loud pop. The gears were grinding as they went prematurely into first gear straight from reverse. Then another maniacal outburst followed by the sound of another collision but this time the crash was metal hitting wood at about five miles per hour.

Hung over guys began waking up and yelling back. I clearly remember someone yelling, "Go to bed yourself," inspiring more maniacal laughter from the driver of the jeep. After winning the jeep duel with the young MABSters CO, our own Clipper was now systematically ramming every Silver Eagles hootch with his damaged jeep.

After another crash, there was pandemonium. I heard the sound of metal clanging as the wall lockers in a nearby hootch fell over. The thuds and crashes continued and were drawing closer to my own hootch. It was clear that Clipper intended to ram all of the hootches if the jeep held out. I heard another metal-on-wood crash. It sounded like the hootch right next

139

to ours. I looked over from my rack to my right through the screen and saw the neighboring hootch sagging sickly.

Before I knew it, the jeep hit our hootch. I was halfway out of the rack when it hit. It missed my corner but the impact was enough to knock me down. My wall locker fell across Maggot's rack. He woke up spitting serious curses. The Fat Maggot slept through it all, having a rack near the back. The front wall of the hootch slumped down in one corner.

I heard the jeep go into reverse and braced myself for another hit but there was only a muffled explosion as the battered engine finally died. I stepped outside. The jeep was in the middle of the company street, a smoking wreck. After the explosion the sounds of steam hissing out and the radiator ticking were all I could hear at first but they were quickly followed by more maniacal laughter.

Almost everybody in the squadron was awake and milling around. Four hootches had taken direct hits from the jeep and were down in one corner. A few had their fronts knocked in, canvas on the ground. Our leader was behind the wheel of the wrecked jeep, drunkenly happy and just minutes from passing out. All across the yard, guys were throwing knocked down gear and water cans out the doors of their wrecked hootches.

I stood there with my hootchmates, amazed as we took a look at the damage. The jeep's engine was smoking and even from 30 feet away I could feel the heat coming off of it. What was most impressive, though, was a tent pole sticking out of the jeep's radiator at an angle. It looked like a cockeyed unicorn's main armament. Apparently in his midnight duel with the boy major, Clipper had veered across someone's front porch and picked up the pole.

Clipper slid clear down to the ground from the driver's opening of the wrecked jeep, got up, looked around and laughed like a possessed loon. He kept mumbling, "You assholes ... wouldn't have a drink with the old man ... showed you, assholes ... ha ha ha...." The boy major had fled back to his own area to rouse out crews to get his dead jeep out of fighter town where the duel had taken place.

Responses ranged from hung-over shock to severe irritation but under it all was some sort of twisted admiration for Clipper. He was our leader. We would gladly follow him. Anywhere. I was not in good enough shape to hang around and see how it all turned out. My bed was still upright and I fell back into it.

Somehow the night section tin-benders from the metal shop under supervision from Beak got Clipper's jeep pushed to the barn. Beak had deep

Chapter 27. Clipper Wins

An unidentified trooper walks away from Clipper's fighter jeep after its repair by the tin-benders, or metalsmiths, following his infamous jeep duel with the MABS boy major. The tin-benders placed scrapped rocket launchers on either side of the jeep and a set of tanker goggles on the hood (*VMFA-115 1972–1973 Silver Eagles Cruise Book*).

admiration for Clipper but not especially for the MABS boy major. Beak left him to repair his own damage. And the hootches weren't really a problem. They were easily fixed. But a wrecked jeep could get the skipper's ass in really hot water. And the big boss Joker didn't have much of a sense of humor regarding off-the-page behavior from his subordinate senior officers.

The tin-benders did first-rate work. In one night, they not only knocked all the dents flush and repainted the scraped metal but they also reupholstered the thing. To add their own special touch, they installed on either side a scrapped two-shot, five-inch rocket launcher and placed a set of tanker's goggles prominently on the hood. Clipper was equipped for his next duel.

I think Clipper took the tin-benders' work as a compliment. The jeep made Clipper the envy of the rest of the Heavies and from what we could tell he avoided any trouble with his boss. We had a photography nut in the squadron and his photo of the restored fighter jeep graces the pages of the *Silver Eagle Cruise Book*. I still have my copy and I cherish it.

***

Section Three—Special Times, Special People

About three months later, we got a package from Laos. Clipper opened it in an All Officers Meeting and read aloud the accompanying letter. Inside the package was a mounted captured North Vietnamese battle flag. The inscription read

HOORAY! To the Silver Eagles of one, one, five, the only people crazy enough to live for years in hootches and then for fun, tear them down. Thanks for a hell of a night.

The Ravens

***

Not long after the meet-up, word came that a Raven had been shot down in the *Plaine des Jarres*. The Raven had put up a fight using his own weapons as the Pathet Lao moved in on him. All available air had gone to try to rescue him but the attempt was unsuccessful.

Worse was to come. The next day, other aircraft, F-4s and Ravens, were working the same target area. The area was cleaned out so that a Raven FAC could fly low and slow over the spot where his brother Raven went down.

What he saw was sickening. The dead Raven had been decapitated and his head was mounted on a long pole near a road junction. From that point on, the war became personal for me and many others. That was what war did.

CHAPTER 28

Christmas

December 1972

One night during a marathon Monopoly game in mid–December 1972, I walked outside the hootch to relieve myself. A three-quarter moon and high thin cirrus clouds were in the sky. Just beneath the lowest cloud level, the moonlit sky was covered with contrails, white streaks oriented north to south. There was not a sound. The cons were from B-52s, headed north for Hanoi and back, one after another.

Later that night, we were awakened by the duty officer and told to report for an All Officers Meeting, where Clipper told us that a huge campaign was on. We would be post-strike re-fuel escorts for the B-52s, the BUFFs. We would be going way north into SAM country, within eyeshot of Hanoi. We should prepare.

As if to punctuate the situation, the next night at 2:00 a.m., a B-52 crash-landed gear up at Nam Phong and slid off the north end of our runway into the red dirt. Apparently, the BUFF took a SAM hit. Part of the rudder was shot away. Since the BUFFs were nuclear-weapons-capable planes, security was strict. That night an armed Air Force security team was sent down from Udorn to cordon off and secure the bird. We were told not to go near it. On pain of being shot.

The next morning as we taxied out for our own hops, we saw a four-foot-tall Eagle, Globe and Anchor, the Marine emblem, artistically applied in gold paint to the black nose and underbelly of the BUFF. So much for Air Force security.

***

I flew 51.6 hours in December 1972. Only two hops were not combat hops. One was a half-hour test hop with an old-school major, callsign Dutch. He wore a flattop haircut and a permanent snarl. The other non-combat hop was with Bantam. He and I flew high and fast across Vietnam, Laos and

Thailand, ferrying our sick bird, unarmed, back to The Rose Garden from Da Nang.

The rest of the month was all red ink, all stops out. Except for Christmas Day. The last thing anyone had thought about was Christmas and all of a sudden there it was.

We were told we would stand down for the day itself. I flew two hops the day before and two hops the day after. Christmas Day was like a hiccup, a flat spot. It was just a day to fill with something other than flying.

That Christmas, I came as close to being a true cynic as I hope I ever come. The NVA and VC were surely not opening presents. The enemy was rearming. Along with every other squadron in the theater, we had been relentlessly pounding the enemy and then we were supposed to give them a day off? I was not alone in my flourishing cynicism or in being angry that we were standing down. The second- and third-tour guys already knew the drill. We were being American, observing Christmas, whether we liked it or not.

***

Around that time, my parents would write fairly often, about every two weeks. Sometimes they recorded eight-track tapes to share their voices and the news from home. I would wait until the hootch was empty, then sit and listen to those tapes. It was a hard thing to do. My parents had no idea of the world I lived and worked in. And I had no plans of telling them. It would have driven my mother to tears and my father would take the blame if anything happened to me. None of us needed that.

For Christmas, they sent me a care package consisting of two items. One was a gallon can of pickled jalapeños. The other was a day-glo-painted black velvet picture from Mexico. It featured a small Mexican kid in gaudy bright yellow clothes and a sombrero. He was dragging behind him a huge empty tequila bottle, his fingers wrapped around it like a toy.

The guys in the hootch thought the picture was the ultimate in awful taste so of course we immediately hung it up. A piece of art like that needed to be available for all to see. The little black-velvet Mexican boy ended up right next to the two-foot-tall Christmas tree made of wire and bottle brushes, sent by another guy's family. We wrapped the tree in one strand of green tinsel. Of course, there were no presents under that tree. It sat squarely in the middle of our only table to show visitors that we had the spirit of Christmas. Ho, Ho, Ho.

Chapter 28. Christmas

Maybe we needed something recognizable after all. After getting our holiday decorations in place, we received a festive invitation on pink paper with heavy blue lines. I suppose that was the closest to red and green available. One of the Silver Eagles had decided that we would have a Christmas party and printed up invites on the squadron's mimeograph machine. On the invite was a caricatured drawing of a feline-looking guy dressed as Santa Claus. True to the season and location, across the top of the invite were bold letters spelling out *Ho Phuqueing Ho*.

At the Christmas party, someone had filled a duty punch bowl full of Christmas cheer—enough 151 rum to light up Cleveland. Our party host had commandeered several plates of GI cookies and some kind soul had seen to it that we had enough Corsicana fruitcakes in their brightly painted tin cans to feed a squadron. No one ate the fruitcakes, including me. But I knew where they were from. I had been to the Collin Street Bakery in Corsicana, Texas, 53 miles from Waco, where I attended university. The tinned fruitcakes started me down a twisting path of over-drinking holiday punch.

I don't know if it was the drinking or the need to have some laughter. Probably both. But at some point, someone opened one of those fruitcake tins. They had been sitting around for several weeks already and the contents were hard as rocks. A friendly game of Christmas fruitcake rolling organically started up. The winner's fruitcake went the farthest. The fruitcakes rolled a little crookedly, more with each additional holiday drink we downed. We had to give them some English when we let them go. We started placing bets and before long we had ourselves a party game.

In between the drinks and laughter, Christmases past would flash in my memory and shine for a moment before disappearing into my subconscious. It was not the best time for reflecting but it would have been poor form not to not join in on the many toasts that went around. I was blearily searching for something I could raise a glass to. I had seen how my own thin religiosity came and went depending on how long it had been since the last inhaling of punch. I wasn't that deep in the joy juice.

But some of us made a try. It was Christmas, after all. José Feliciano had released a version of *"Feliz Navidad"* that got a lot of play that night. That particular version always takes me back to that peculiar Christmas.

The last order of partying was the singing of carol parodies from a songbook that mysteriously appeared. They were some of the raunchiest, funniest barracks ballads ever sung and they have been passed on from one generation of young men who flew in combat to the next lucky group. The one that sticks in my mind was called "Silver Bombs." That Christmas night, we sang them all and went to bed.

***

Flying and bombing started up again on 26 December.

CHAPTER 29

The Chapel

January 1973

Just to the west of the cluster of hootches known as Group Headquarters was what passed as the Chapel of The Rose Garden. It was an empty Southeast Asia hut—the only one in Nam Phong that was painted white. The pews were backless, freestanding plain wooden benches. The floors were the same as the ones we lived on, rough teak plywood, usually unswept. The altar and pulpit, such as they were, had been made from empty five-inch Zuni rocket crates. They were well carpentered, the American pine sanded smooth. Except for some black stenciling on the inside of the pulpit, it too was painted white.

Out front stood a cross about five feet tall, made of two-by-fours also painted white. At its foot was a small cluster of rosebushes, two or three, that the padres had sent over. They had tanked the dirt up around the roses in a circle to hold irrigation water. Next to the rosebushes was a white Protestant-looking sign in the ground with *Chapel of The Rose Garden* stenciled in black paint. Except for the roses, the hard, red sand surrounding the chapel area was absent of any ground cover, just like everything else.

***

To be honest, we didn't think of the chaplains much until we lost somebody or unless someone had a family emergency back in the world, urgent situations. According to Marine regulations, we had two chaplains assigned to us, both Naval Officers, one Protestant, one Catholic. We called both of them padre. The mackerel-snapper padre, the Roman Catholic priest, could hold his liquor. The RC was tough and young and would drink with anybody.

The Protestant padre, I wasn't so sure about. On his party suit, he had a cross embroidered at an angle in gold thread. For a long time, I thought it was a tilted Martini glass, a strange insignia for a minister. He was a nice enough guy. We would see him at Happy Hours, trying to be happy. He got buzzed pretty early and pretty often. To me, he seemed to not really be there, to not really *want* to be there. As if he was treading spiritual water.

I had been raised Baptist. I was curious to see how someone who bought into all the American Protestant Christianity stuff would handle it in the middle of the killing, destruction and loss that surrounded us. I shadowed the Protestant chaplain at Happy Hour one night. I wondered what he would talk about with a few Nam Phong cocktails in his stomach. I do not remember what he said.

***

It wasn't until we had a long lull in the bombing—when the chaplains knew we would have a whole weekend off—that they button-holed us and politicked us to go to church. During such a lull in January 1973, we had time on our hands. We had been spooled up to a high tempo of operations, so during the lull we entertained ourselves through reading, board games, running, football, volleyball and poker.

But sometimes the simple distractions weren't enough. We all were missing *something,* were all kind of uneasy. We had too much time to think. Without constant flying, I felt as if I was walking under water again, going through the motions slowly, laboriously. At a jungle-rules volleyball game one Saturday afternoon, I heard Beak was planning to go to the chapel the next morning. The padres had been working the boys pretty hard that day at lunch.

Since Beak was a Heavy, I thought that some of our other senior officers would feel compelled to go too, to act as good examples for the rest of us. I decided to tag along. On that Sunday morning, I went to the chapel mostly out of curiosity. At the appointed time, 40 of us tramped in. The congregation was all men, all Marines, officers and enlisted. In the chapel that day, I saw men I didn't know well but whose faces were familiar. They were our support guys from the Force Service Support Group. They were tough-looking, slitty-eyed, grizzled old men with lined faces. To a man, they were stout with broad shoulders. The type of Marine who didn't take guff from anyone regardless of rank. They were all Marine captains, many of them Mustangs. They were weary from their responsibilities and the knowledge that the whole thing really did depend on them as professionals. Rumpled and sweat-streaked, they wore full jungle utilities complete with blouse. We thought of them as grunts, ground pounders, infantry. But then to us, anyone who didn't fly was a grunt.

***

Chapter 29. The Chapel

I walked in early and took a seat. I heard the sound of jungle boots respectfully shuffling across the plywood floor as the last men quietly came into the chapel. Nobody spoke though the backless benches audibly groaned under the strain of so much human weight.

When the Protestant padre realized that everyone was inside, he remained silent. He just gazed and, in his gazing, communicated.

It was the deepest quiet I had encountered since arriving at The Rose Garden. It was the devastating quiet of a bunch of self-conscious men for whom this type of silence was out of character. The padre went with it and his eyes stayed on us. He made himself wait. I could tell. It was almost like he was waiting for us to tell him what to do. He was unsure. The silence in the chapel was a living silence, moving around.

It was quiet outside as well, no jet engines turning up to make noise and break the silent tension. We were all feeling awkward. I furtively looked around, head bowed in a half-remembered Lord's Prayer that I never finished. It was incongruity right up in my face, our faces. When the padre cleared his throat, it signaled that the curious worship service was about to begin.

The padre asked Beak to open with a prayer. Beak stood, all six-feet-Texas-two of him dressed in jungle utilities, to offer a prayer. The church was restless now, shifting, but still quiet. Beak kept his eyes shut tight with the knowledge that every man was listening. He lost me after he said the first *Heavenly Father* but at least the tension was gone. We read a responsive reading from the back of a very worn maroon government-issued hymnal. Once we finished, the maroon covers were closed in unison, sending puffs of dust flying into the air, swirling around us and adding to the oddness of the situation.

***

The bone honesty of it got to me—grown men earnestly trying to connect to something, to figure out in their confusion *how* to worship. For heaven's sake or hell's bells, we were flying combat hops yesterday and would again tomorrow. I was witnessing truly tough and hardened grown men making an effort in the best, the only way they knew how. Because something in them said *Be there*.

There was no social cachet that went with attending—no mothers, fathers, wives, or children expecting them to be there, *at church*. No. They didn't *have* to be there. They wanted to be there, maybe needed to be there

149

for whatever reason. The sermon was forgettable. The singing from the maroon hymnals was strained, forced and off key.

At the end, there was a scooting of benches as we all rose for the benediction. The final amen from the padre signaled the start of another heavy shuffle of boots heading out the screen door and back into the hot bright day. Covers went back on heads and smokers fired up their butts. Nobody stayed to tell the padre that he had given a good sermon. Nobody said anything. There was nothing to say.

***

When I ran into Beak at our one and only Silver Eagles reunion, I mentioned this church service to him. I told him that I had not been to a more meaningful church service before or since. He said he hadn't either. Neither of us really knew why but we both remembered it.

CHAPTER 30

The Brig

March 1973

The jungle of north central Thailand was always hot but this afternoon it seemed particularly so. My tour had been split. In my new role as Group buildings and grounds officer, I was walking my duty rounds. My title was a crude joke because the buildings were 95 percent canvas tents over plywood floors and the grounds were hardened dirt. But the Marine Corps had its standing orders and its pre-ordained job assignments.

I was checking that all the troopers' hootches had fire extinguishers or water cans and recording those that did not. In my wandering, I ended up in the grunt area where the infantry was hootched. Their area was further down the hill from the aviation area because they did not have to walk up and back to the flight line to work every day as the wingers did. I was a winger so I didn't usually come to the infantry area. But in my Group role with the senior operational command as the public works guy, I was responsible for monitoring the infantry quarters in The Rose Garden.

Everything was acceptable. In fact, the grunt troopers kept their area in better shape than the wingers did. Marine infantry are fastidious about their living spaces—at sea, in barracks or in the jungle—just as long as they aren't being shot at. The infantry manned our wire but no hostiles ever tried to penetrate it. A tiger did one night. We thought we were being overrun and brought the .50-calibers to life but the tiger wasn't injured.

As a battalion—the infantry equivalent of an aviation squadron—the infantry at the Garden had a platoon of military police, MPs, who were in charge of keeping the peace inside the confines of the base. I had heard they had a brig but had not toured it yet. I figured I would check it out. It was a building of sorts after all.

I could see the brig from a distance. It was actually a metal shipping container, referred to as a Conex box—about seven feet high, twelve feet long and eight feet wide. Conex boxes were made of heavy gauge sheet metal. They were originally designed to be carried in ships' cargo holds or lashed to the decks with steel cables. This makeshift brig had five-inch wide slats cut out with a welder's torch between the ribs of the metal box to serve as vents. At one end of the box, a barn-type door opened out on hinges. The door could be shut and secured with a single heavy locking arm and clevis with a large metal lock.

The thought of a man in that box under the jungle sun seemed almost too severe, almost a type of torture. Anything made of metal exposed to that sub-tropical sun became too hot to touch in minutes. I could not imagine what the temperature reached inside even if the floor was not in direct sunlight. Not that Marine brigs were ever known for their hospitality but this set-up verged on cruel and unusual. On the other hand, the unofficial expeditionary orders were to make do with what we had.

About ten feet away from the brig building, four full-height telephone poles were set at the corners, tops angled in. The poles were wrapped round with numerous rolls of razored concertina wire, forming a fence at least ten-feet high. I couldn't tell how the MPs entered the wire fence to open or close the door to the brig so I walked around to take a closer look. My timing was not good. I heard activity on the back side of the brig and as I walked around, I saw the source.

Just outside the wire fence, two white MPs were trying to subdue an African American Marine and get him inside the fence surrounding the Conex-box brig. The African American Marine was a big man wearing only jungle utility trousers and boots, bare-chested and uncovered. He was handcuffed but fighting fiercely to keep from being put in that box. The MPs had the advantage in number and, I had to presume, in the force of law. Neither was as large as the prisoner but both had night sticks and were using them. Later, I learned that regulations called for passive use of force when subduing an unarmed, handcuffed man. That meant no hits above the shoulders. To the MPs' credit, if credit could ever be given in a scene like that, I saw no blows above the shoulders.

The prisoner was fighting a losing battle. He would duck the blows or lean and feint away as best he could but then the MP on the other side would deliver a blow. One MP tried to wrestle him to the ground. The prisoner let out a loud low-toned hoarse sound and the blows continued. Both the MP and the prisoner went down into the dirt. The man got up quickly, his face covered with red dust where he had hit the ground. The MP had also rolled in the dust, his usually squared-away jungle utility uniform now askew and also coated with the powdery red dust.

The prisoner's groans rose to a long, low howl and a line of thick slobber and spittle began to fling from his mouth and nose as he horsed himself around, continuing to try to break free. The sound of those night sticks hitting heavy solid blows against that man's bared flesh and bone was sickening. When wood and bone made contact, the cracking sound was distinct. I can still hear that sound now. The sight of the man being beaten, for whatever reason, forced to the ground, and slowly struggling to get back up just to be beaten down again eviscerated me. My stomach knotted and I had to fight to keep from gagging.

I watched for more than a minute and not one look of notice was given to me standing there. I didn't move a muscle or say a word. I walked away sickened and angry.

Later, I would ask many questions but right then I had no authority whatsoever to interfere in MP matters. The MPs were doing their jobs. They had information I did not have.

***

Racism was a reality in Vietnam. I may not have actually thought about racism that day but what did flash in my mind, rightly or wrongly, was that this had to be what slavery might have looked like at times. White overseers punishing an errant slave. I knew that wasn't what I had witnessed but the thought flashed in my mind anyway. It seared itself in. I was from the South and I knew history.

Behind or underneath or woven through the reality of racism was the Marine Corps' reliance on discipline—a discipline that in general was different among air wingers than it was for infantry. That difference didn't help this matter. Air wingers were focused on getting airplanes in an up-status to fly missions, to drop bombs or to shoot down MiGs. We needed intelligent enlisted men trained in science-based disciplines or capable of being trained technically. Not men oriented toward launching bullets, passing inspections, saluting or having spit-shined boots. All Marines learned how to do these things in boot camp. And damned right, there was and is a need for them. But a fighter squadron was not an infantry operation where traditional military discipline was the order of the day.

Salutes between officers and enlisted were exchanged as long as both were covered (wearing uniform caps), and they were not in the field. As often as not, our enlisted went about uncovered. On the flight line, by regulation and for safety reasons, maintenance men were *required* to be uncovered. No one wanted a cap with a metal insignia on it sucked down the intake of a J-79 engine. That could wreck the plane. It had happened. And as a rule, officers did not salute each other because salutes could enable a sniper off in the jungle to identify and shoot the higher-ranking officers.

There was a quirk to aviation. In the air wing, the officers were actually *fighting* the war. There was a solid bridge of trust between our enlisted who repaired and maintained the planes and the officers who flew them. We *knew* those men. They *knew* us. We knew they looked up to us in a way but we also knew our lives on every single hop were in their hands. They knew it too. We had to get along, more than get along. And we didn't let over-rigid adherence to spit, polish and minor matters of military discipline interfere with mission accomplishment.

Among the infantry, the approach was different. In the infantry, where the enlisted do the bulk of the actual fighting and the officers direct it, rigid military discipline in big and small matters was the order of the day. Junior officers often fought too. But the infantry depended on noncommissioned officers and junior enlisted to accomplish its mission.

Thus, the infantry came down hard on dotting i's and crossing t's. Passing inspections and respecting authority were *de rigueur*. Insubordination of any degree was not tolerated.

***

I will never know what the struggling prisoner did to deserve being put in the brig in the first place but I know that he must have committed a serious infraction. It could have been disciplinary in nature, such as insubordination. It could have been criminal.

Something of what I saw that day was badly wrong. But something of it may not have been. All of it made my stomach turn.

CHAPTER 31

The Shadow Next Door

1972–1973

Shadow was a member of VMFA-232, the Red Devils. I was a member of VMFA-115, the Silver Eagles. Our squadrons were stationed side by side at The Rose Garden. The Silver Eagles jokingly referred to the Red Devils as *the girls next door* and they referred to us in the same way. A kind of looser, probably sexist language that was part of our lives in 1972. Many junior officers, like Shadow and me, knew each other across squadrons. We had been mutually stationed in the States on the East Coast and during the war, we shared liberty time together away from the prying ears of the Heavies.

Shadow's squadron flew a newer model of the Phantom, the F-4 J, while my squadron flew the older F-4 B model. The J had stronger engines, a newer radar and wider tires. Because 232 flew the newer plane, one night at a fairly drunken Happy Hour their commanding officer mocked Clipper and the Silver Eagles by referring to our F-4s as *them old airplanes with them skinny tires.* Clipper kept his cool and didn't fire back that while 115 had not lost a plane out of The Rose Garden, 232 had lost two by that time.

One 232 F-4 ran out of gas and flamed out short of The Rose Garden. That plane was a loss but the aircrew survived. A second 232 Phantom had been shot down by a MiG primarily because of a lack of knowledge and proficiency. The plane had not jettisoned its external fuel tanks or increased its speed, as was standard procedure for a fight. In my opinion, the event was a failure of leadership in the air. While the RIO got away due to a successful joint-service effort, the pilot was never recovered.

Lest there be any doubt, despite the inter-squadron bickering and posturing, when the chips were down or one of the planes went down from our neighboring Nam Phong squadrons, 232 or 533, all Marine air turned to, flew to the scene and did everything possible to help out brother Marines. In fact, when a third 232 plane was shot down later, VMFA-115 planes flew over the area where the bird was downed for so long they almost ran out of gas trying to keep the bad guys off.

155

Section Three—Special Times, Special People

That night in the bar, it would have been poor form to bring up loss records. But when the head Red Devil kept up the trash talk, Clipper walked over to where our squadron guys had gathered and observed all of this. He snarled to us, "Those are fighting words." We duly noted Clipper's position and promised ourselves to show up our rivals, peacefully, as often as we could. Volleyball, flag football, or tiddlywinks.

At Happy Hour, junior officers also spent bar time in serious talk about things that happened and why they happened. We talked about our Heavies. The quiet consensus was that 115 was lucky in having Clipper as our CO and 232 was unlucky with its commanding officer, who apparently was interested mostly in making his next rank and impressing people—a good, tight, proficient squadron be damned. Shadow and I had these talks in passing. At The Rose Garden, we had to watch what we said and had to be loyal to our own outfits. Unit loyalty in the Marine Corps was and is paramount.

Later in our checkered careers, post–Vietnam, Shadow and I ended up in the same F-4 Reserve squadron, VMFA-112 out of Naval Air Station Dallas. In private conversation during deployments or on cross-country flights or in O-Club bars or even the ready room, we rehashed our time during that last year of the war. No trips down memory lane business. But it helped us both to deal with what we experienced there. Free from the many distractions of those times, we compared notes on circumstances and people, what went down, what we learned. I realized Shadow and I had a support group of two. Only those who were there could get it. We had to corroborate for each other. Much of what we talked of cannot be shared. Not even closest family would understand.

What I can share is that after The Rose Garden days, Shadow got off active duty and tried his hand at being an airline pilot. He kept flying as a reservist through two or more career changes and ended up doing very well. He attained senior rank and became one of the best commanding officers I ever served and flew under. In part, I became a Heavy because of what I learned from Shadow, starting in The Rose Garden.

What we shared were accurate templates on how to lead well and, as importantly, how not to lead well. We learned above all, the value of individual Marines, officer and enlisted. How important, then and now, their lives are. Eventually, we both had enough of the regular Marine Corps but we were and are still deeply attached to it. And we loved and still love flying.

CHAPTER 32

Salts

1972–1973

In the field of medicine, there is a saying, *See one. Do one. Teach one.* Probably true in some way for people in any job or career. First, you watch and learn from the experts. Next, you test yourself, finding out for sure that you have mastered your craft. And if you have not, what you need to learn. If you have, then you can move on to the *teach one* phase, supervising, mentoring, passing along what you have learned. And the cycle repeats.

In Marine Corps talk, we have the *fucking new guys*, the FNGs, who come into their roles after stringent training, to be sure, but find themselves short on experience. If they are lucky, the FNGs are taken under the wings of the *salts*, often older and always more experienced Marines, who watch the newbies, correct their mistakes, answer their questions. Those FNGs may indeed become salts themselves, though not all do. Only some evolve into the most seasoned and respected.

As an FNG myself, I was fortunate to learn from some of the saltiest salts. Men I learned to respect as Marines and as people. Later I too became salty, maybe not to the degree of some of my mentors but I did assume the role of helping along a new crop of FNGs. *Fucking new guy* is a Marine aviation variant on the Naval aviation term *nugget*, a newly winged, first-tour Naval flyer. Perhaps *nugget* refers to the small, single gold bar that is the rank insignia of an ensign in the Navy or a second lieutenant in the Marine Corps. There was even a Marine RIO whose callsign was FUNGUS, fucked-up new guy under supervision.

My dad, a Navy veteran, taught me that the term *salt* also comes from the Navy as a traditional name for a sailor who has made at least one cruise aboard ship, maybe more. It is akin to *tar* from the days of *iron men and wooden ships* when sailors would return from a cruise with tar, used for caulking the seams of wooden ships, in their hair and on their clothing.

We were all FNGs at one time. I certainly was and I made my share of new guy mistakes. And I was extremely lucky to know salts who made a big difference in my career. In my life. By rank and experience, Clipper was the saltiest in VMFA-115. His skill, wisdom, and street smarts fill the pages of this book as they filled my days in The Rose Garden. I could mention several more but here are stories of three other salts who helped this FNG.

***

January 1973. At an AOM in The Rose Garden, Clipper was reading off names of inbound replacement RIOs and asked if we knew any of them. When I heard Suitcase's name I said, "He's a good one." I told Clipper later about how Suitcase had helped me. "If Suitcase had not spent his own time off to work with me," I said, "I would never have gotten my wings."

Suitcase checked into VMFA-115 for another tour in Wes-Pac shortly after that AOM, but before he was cleared for combat he needed a check ride. He had been out of the F-4 for two years. I asked flight ops that Suitcase be on my wing for his check ride. For that one hop, he was my FNG but he had no problem at all. After the check ride, he asked me his grade. I laughed and said, "You got a hard *up*." I gave him the best grade he could get.

"Damned good thing," he said, "because I'm your new ground boss." He had taken over administration, where I worked as assistant awards officer at that time. I had known Suitcase years before. I had just completed the training unit called VT-10 in Pensacola, Florida, where I learned to navigate an airplane and read a map in the air and where I was introduced to flying in a jet. I then was ordered to Naval Air Station, Glynco, Georgia, where I would learn to read radar and run an intercept in the air between our fighters and the bogey. All of this would take place in a three-dimensional world rather that the two-dimensional training world I was used to.

I knew this school was the acid test. If I successfully completed it, I would get my wings and go on to fly Phantoms in a fleet gun squadron. If I washed out, I would wait around until the Marine Corps figured out what to do with me.

On my first day of class, Suitcase, a senior captain and recent Vietnam returnee, gave the orientation talk. He was a big man. All business, strictly Marine. After laying out the course work in training blocks, he made it very clear that this school would take lots of work as we learned a new iteration of flying. Three downs, or failed hops, and we would be out. Suitcase would be a grader on some of the training hops and told us we could come to him if we just couldn't get a clue.

After we completed our familiarization or fam rides and got down to graded hops, I was as lost as lost could be. I tentatively approached Suitcase in the hall one day and told him my clue bag was empty. His dictum was *think ahead of the airplane* but I was stuck on the ground. He told me to come in on Saturday and we would work in the trainer. I lost count of the Saturdays I spent at that trainer with Suitcase.

One day he taught me intercept geometry as we took turns running and pedaling on bicycles that he had brought to the parking lot. Then back into the sub, our name for the trainer, to work the intercepts out on radar. The hardest thing for me to grasp was the concept of target aspect, how many degrees were in the angle that the bogey saw you from. But Suitcase had a gift for simplifying things that seemed opaque.

Toward the end of the school, he told me and the other delinquents he'd worked with on Saturdays that we'd done well so we were going on another kind of work trip. To an orphanage way out near St. Simon's Island. We were going to help him rehab it. We cleaned chicken coops, hoed weeds, hauled wood and generally cleaned it up. That was work I could do, having grown up agrarian.

The show time was nearing for wings or no wings. I failed one hop but flew a makeup with Suitcase and on 21 January 1971, got my golden wings. He absolutely made a difference in my life. After our time in Nam Phong, we didn't stay in touch. But I carry his influence with me still even though he died in a mid-air training collision in 1980. A day I lost one of my saltiest mentors.

***

I came to admire another salty RIO, callsign Ducks, much later. I nick-named him Ducks myself because of his ducktail hairstyle, which he wore slicked down with Brylcreem or something like it. Ducks had longish hair for a senior captain. Usually Mustang captains wore very short hair. But hair regulations in the Marine Corps were not strictly adhered to, except for grunts. Anyway, I got the distinct feeling Ducks was too old to worry about too much.

I clearly remember a conversation we had one afternoon late after everyone else had gone to chow. I went into his office in The Rose Garden's operations hootch, just to bat the breeze. He was sitting at his desk looking over his flight gear. I had flown that day and had just taken off my pack, trying to relax. Ducks was an F-4 J RIO and flew with VMFA-232. He looked tired, as he usually did. But the lines on his face seemed deeper than I remembered and he was not talkative. When I asked if he had a night hop, the memorable part of our conversation began.

159

He stood up and looked me straight in the eye. "I don't really want this hop and you are a B guy and can't take it. I am through with wanting to fly. I have done enough. I'll keep doing it but the fun in it is long gone. You have to know when enough is enough. And that is where I am."

He shouldered his flight gear and, like the professional he was, began the walk over to 232's flight line to take his hop. Here was a career man, had started enlisted, become a warrant, then got commissioned. He had flown three hard tours in Vietnam. By the time we met, his job had lost its charm.

Gaper, a fellow retired RIO, recently handed me a book about a Marine pilot we both knew of. I, in fact, had met this pilot in civilian times. The book is titled *Into the Tiger's Jaw, America's First Black Marine Aviator, The Autobiography of Lt. Gen. Frank E. Petersen,* written with J. Alfred Phelps. I took the book home and began reading it. I knew several names in it, places, things about Vietnam, but I was not prepared to read of Ducks, who had been in the same squadron and had flown with Lt. Gen. Petersen. I learned about a hop when they were shot down and injured after ejection and a rough landing in a highly contested, lethal place in Vietnam.

I thought back to that conversation Ducks and I had in The Rose Garden. Older men who had been in the F-4 their whole lives did not tell many war stories even to us who were in combat with them. Of course, he would be tired and war weary. But he would stay the course, even knowing much more about what could happen than most of us would ever know. Ducks passed away a few years ago, peacefully, not in a time of war.

***

He Coon was the saltiest RIO I ever knew. And one of the finest men. I first knew him at Cherry Point where he was aviation maintenance officer in my squadron, VMFA-312, and therefore my boss. He was a senior captain filling a billet that usually required a major according to the Marine Corps Table of Organization.

He Coon had flown in the Phantom ever since there were Phantoms. He began his career in the Marine Corps as an enlisted man, becoming a warrant officer (RO, radar observer) before the government decided commissioned officers were needed in the back seats. For nuclear capability, we were told. He Coon did what was necessary to bootstrap up and get a commission and transition to RIO. He knew the Marine Corps inside and out and especially knew the value of people as persons. Including how to treat properly those who outranked him and still make his point, get what he needed. He was an astute judge of character.

160

Chapter 32. Salts

He Coon knew everything about the Phantom and about radar, including how to run a perfect intercept, which was what the Phantom was built to do. Or what to do in any emergency. He came to VMFA-312 when it was basically on its ass. More birds were down for repairs than were up in the air. He also stepped in when we had a very mediocre CO who tried to micromanage the maintenance work. As He Coon's maintenance control officer, only one year into my Marine career, I was responsible for getting enough birds into an up-status to meet the next day's flight schedule. The often-drunken CO would call me at home, sometimes at 2:00 a.m., offering suggestions on how to do my job. He Coon put a stop to that and told the CO to call *him* instead.

He also advised me quietly to get out of that squadron. It was going nowhere under that particular CO and the war was still going on. The Easter offensive had started up in 1972 in Vietnam and He Coon knew RIOs would be needed. Quotas began coming down to F-4 squadrons. He Coon said if I put in for the next opening, he and Driver, a friend of his who was a Heavy, would help me get it. They knew the intricacies of the system and I got my orders.

The day He Coon arrived at The Rose Garden, I saw him walking dead tired down the company street. I insisted he come in and take over my bed in the hootch. By this time, The Fat Maggot had taken a FAC tour over to Okinawa and we had room. He Coon was on his third tour of the war when he got to Nam Phong in 1973. The first two tours were based in-country, in Vietnam. He Coon finished the war with a total of 545 combat missions, a Distinguished Flying Cross, 38 Air Medals for routine combat hops, and a Single Mission Air Medal for outstanding performance on a single hop. In contrast, I had 131 combat hops and got eight Air Medals. A big difference.

I owe He Coon much as a boss. To this day, he is the best of examples in the Marine Corps and out.

***

Few RIO's in Uncle Sam's Misguided Children, the USMC, could have had better flying salts to learn from than I did. Keep in mind, none of these salts was a perfect officer or RIO or man, by any stretch. They would all laugh if they even knew I had mentioned them here. Or they would get upset. But their intersections in my Marine Corps life were significant then, as they were later in my life after the Marine Corps. They left their stamps, all of them.

Things Changed

CHAPTER 33

Squadron to Group

March–August 1973

In January 1973, *Stars and Stripes,* the quasi-governmental newspaper, carried the news in a bold-print headline that the war was over. Although few of us really believed that, we held a The-War-Is-Over-Party replete with steaks and booze. We stood down for about a week and then began again flying combat hops in Laos. Legally, we presumed. Roughly two weeks later, we were also ordered to fly combat hops in Cambodia as well. But no longer in Vietnam proper. We *now* know of the infamous killing fields of Cambodia and the murder of thousands of innocents but at the time we did not. I wanted to believe. I took for granted we were going against the right targets.

My steady flying kept up until the end of March. By then I had five months left until my rotation date. Back to the world. But before then, it was my time for the split in my tour.

***

Though we didn't like to think about it, rumors tinged with reality always floated around that our tours were likely to be split, which meant a reassignment from our primary job in the cockpit to a different job out of the cockpit for part of the tour. The non-cockpit part of a split might come at the beginning, the middle or the end of the tour.

For Naval Aviators or Naval Flight Officers, the split tour could mean becoming a ground-FAC or an air liaison officer with the infantry. The needs of the Marine Corps trumped personal preference or original assignment. Men I knew had previously served such non-cockpit splits with the infantry when the ground war in Vietnam was at its most intense. These splits were mandated because the Marine Corps had learned that in effectively integrated air-ground combat operations, it was essential to have a flyer on the ground with the infantry combatants. My hootchmate The Fat Maggot had already been sent to Okinawa to serve a split with the infantry.

A strong suit uniquely Marine was its practice and expertise in close air support. Air wingers were there primarily to support Marines or allies on the ground. The ground FAC or air liaison officer could speak *airplane*—knew what a battle area looked like from the air, knew what planes could and couldn't do and could help put the right kind of ordnance where it was most effective.

I had the qualifying training for ground-FAC noted in my record book. I had that military occupational specialty, MOS, had been formally school-trained for it. By the time my orders for Wes-Pac came, RIOs were required to attend this school and become designated for it before shoving off.

But my own tour split in a different way. I found out about my reassignment from my new boss, a major, callsign Rat, who gave me the bad news at a not-so-happy Happy Hour on a Friday afternoon. My split was not from the cockpit to the infantry but from a fighter squadron to Marine Air Group 15 Headquarters as the embarkation officer, with other collateral duties as needed.

I would be the one on whom the entire retrograde would hinge—the move out of Nam Phong of all MAG-15 and its attached units. Or so I egotistically thought. Of course, I would have help but it would be a task of magnitude any way I sliced it. When I got the news, I was angry and felt betrayed. I knew the futility of those feelings but they were still very strong. I would become a *groupie*, in the parlance of the flyers. I would no longer be a Silver Eagle RIO first. The news was tempered somewhat because I knew I could snivel the odd hop with the Silver Eagles. I also knew very well that going to Group was indeed better than going grunt.

Rat knew the impact of the reassignment. His own tour had been split at the start. He had been assured that he was to hold a responsible position in a gun squadron but when he checked in, he had been re-assigned to head Group S-4, Logistics. As soon as he got the word, he had gone off to drink it down. He suggested I do the same.

To make me feel better about my split, he assured me that the retrograde, the move out of Nam Phong, would not happen on my watch. He had written the retrograde order, called Operation Sunset, himself. He swore I would rotate back stateside before it came. He even made me a twenty-dollar bet to that effect. We shook on it. That was a big deal because regardless of rank, officers—then gentlemen by Act of Congress—stood up to gambling debts. Rat also chuckled and said that having him for my boss would be good for my career. That was a throw-away line used thousands of times by senior officers to juniors.

Chapter 33. Squadron to Group

Nonetheless, news of my split tour stung. For the only time in my 31 years as a Marine officer, I cried. In front of our ops officer Fish. Tears of anger. My split was from the fighter squadron to the MAG-15 staff with a specific assignment to the S-4 logistics shop, primarily as embarkation officer, yes, but with ground safety, and buildings and grounds officer as my second and third jobs. The Marine Corps Table of Organization for an Air Group required an officer for each of these billets so on paper I was holding three Group jobs as a first lieutenant. My counterparts in the Air Force and Army were majors. They had trouble accepting my lower rank but always treated me as an equal to my face.

The S-4 shop ordinarily caught all the work that enabled groups and squadrons to fly their missions. Jet fuel, oxygen, nitrogen, missiles, C-rations, bombs, rockets, spare engine parts, waste disposal, drinking water, the dispensary, the doctors, chaplains, road tar, electricity, cooks, hootches and even a fire department. S-4 was responsible for it all.

We were lucky to have a Marine Air Base Squadron attached to Marine Air Group 15.

In civilian parlance, Colonel Joker was the mayor of our little Rose Garden town, Major Rat was the city manager and I was the public works director. I monitored the upkeep of the whole camp. I had gone from Shitty Little Jobs Officer of a squadron to SLJO of a Group. Now I oversaw the removal of actual shit instead of the making of coffee.

On the Monday morning after I got the reassignment news, I reported to Group Headquarters, or the head-shed, and got my desk. I met the guys I would be working for and with. A highly capable, hardnosed Mustang captain and pilot, callsign Agile, was Rat's assistant. I was the sole lieutenant in a sea of Heavies. We also had a gunnery sergeant, or gunny, and a staff sergeant fresh off his tour as a drill instructor at Parris Island, South Carolina. The team was rounded out by an assortment of privates, PFCs and lance corporals.

During my time at Group, I came to know one of the lance corporals, who was one of the best Marines I ever worked with. I nicknamed him Morgan Horse. He didn't have a callsign because he was not aircrew. He was a quiet young man, almost shy, efficient and totally conscientious. His work was always done. He never shirked a responsibility. His military appearance was always squared away and he was always quick with the *Yes, sirs* and *No, sirs*. In later years, as I wound my way through the Marine Corps, often stumbling, I would laugh to myself at how this lance corporal had taught me as much about professionalism as any commissioned officer I served with.

He was not comfortable fraternizing with an officer but we did talk a few times. He was from upstate New York and his family raised Morgan horses. Our agricultural families gave us some common ground.

The S-4 shop had no corporals—the lowest ranking NCO—to act as a buffer between the enlisted and their immediate senior, our one staff sergeant, who had a corrosive approach to Marine life in general. He was tough on the younger troopers. A tour on the drill field did that to him. I would step in from time to time to run interference for the younger miscreant troopers.

One such interference concerned an enlisted man who had married a prostitute in Udorn and had gone *unauthorized absence*, UA, for a while. Without trying to work with the man at all or counsel him in any way, the staff sergeant wrote up the enlisted man for a summary court-martial. With not too much investigating, I learned that the man was deeply in love with his wife or thought he was. He did have to face the consequences of his action but he also needed guidance and help taking care of his new spouse. The padres worked on the counseling side. I worked on a punishment appropriate to his strike-one offense. The man forfeited a month's pay and got appropriate low proficiency and conduct marks but did not face court-martial.

This kind of duty didn't fall under my embarkation, ground safety or building and grounds responsibilities but it did fall under commissioned seniority. I served a purpose and I felt proper about it. By now, my flight time had seriously dwindled. The hops went to squadron guys, as they should have. That still bothered me, although not as much as I thought it would. I already had my coveted 100-mission patch and besides, I had more than enough do to.

I even went so far as to turn down non-combat training hops although I would never even *think* of dodging a combat hop. I wanted red ink. That was what I went over for. I hadn't gone to Nam Phong to burn fuel peacefully boring holes in the sky. Sniveling out of training hops was my way at getting back at the system that had sent me to Group in the first place. And flying wasn't as much fun without my old original gang. The group of guys I had cared about and measured myself against had been broken up bit by bit by the ending of tours. The hard cores who ran the Silver Eagles were rotating out of combat in ones and twos.

Unit rotation as we know it today did not appear until decades later when some genius finally quantified unit rotation efficiency and found it higher than piecemealing individuals into and out of combat. The whole bunch goes, the whole bunch comes back. Together.

Chapter 33. Squadron to Group

Clipper's own replacement had shown up by then and Clipper had his hands full allaying fears that the squadron would turn to shit without him. Good officer that he was, he lied and told us his replacement would be better than he was. Ha. The replacement wasn't. There was only one Clipper.

***

While we waited for Operation Sunset to activate, Joker wanted to improve the raggedy-ass standard of living in Nam Phong. No one watched out for us except us. Our own Wing Headquarters wouldn't re-supply us. They had standing orders to leave a stash of things packed-up intact *in case we went to war*. Ironic, huh? The mysterious untouchable *ninety-day pack-up*. Everything in the pack-up was what we needed and couldn't have. Wing owned us but they couldn't or wouldn't take care of us. Task Force Delta couldn't help us with the Wing problem because we and they were on Temporary Additional Duty, TAD, orders. They probably knew something we didn't know. Like we were soon to come home.

We had to take care of ourselves. As the Group buildings and grounds guy, I was tasked to find any stuff that could improve our lot. I had the best scrounging teacher I could have had in a senior S-4 captain from the Silver Eagles, callsign Mach-Mach, an old-school RIO. He taught me, among other things, that every time we landed in Da Nang to refuel, rearm, and eat, we should take advantage of the opportunity to scrounge. From Mach-Mach, I learned to do whatever it took.

We should sign some phony-ass name to a requisition document, strap in, be ready to go and then let our troopers fill up the backseat all around us with as many boots, skivvies, jungle utilities, tee shirts, blankets and poncho liners—whatever—as the plane could hold. We were out of everything at The Rose Garden. The U.S. Army was giving that stuff away to the Army of the Republic of Vietnam, ARVN. We knew instinctively Marines came first, so the made-up and thus hard-to-find Second Lieutenant Joe Bonnotz signed for one hell of a lot of gear. So did his stepbrother Second Lieutenant Grabbasanwitch. Different fathers.

Since we always flew a combat hop on the way back to the Garden from Da Nang, we could imagine the newspaper headline if one of the re-supply birds got hit. It would read something like *Marine Phantom full of skivvies and poncho liners hit by anti-aircraft artillery*. Or *300 Viet Cong estimated wounded by falling jungle boots and smothered by clothing and blankets*.

Forgiveness for scrounging tactics was easy to obtain, especially when I got my boss a new pair of jungle boots that actually fit. Permission, however, was not so easy to obtain, so I operated accordingly. By then, Joker realized what I was up against and called me into his office one day. He had me write my own set of orders, which he signed. He told me to go where I needed to go and authorized me to use Military Airlift Command, or Air Force transport. A huge deal for a mere first lieutenant. Attached to the orders, the Joker even gave me a list of exactly what he wanted. Now, I could legally transport all the stuff I could scrounge back to the Garden. My orders made me an *official unofficial scrounger*.

Next, I needed to know what *malls* to shop in. The advice I got was to forget the Navy. They were as poor as we were. I should go Air Force or Army bases, in that order. To their salvage yards. After asking around, I was told that Clark AFB in the Philippines was like a supply depot for Wes-Pac of things junked by the USAF. Apparently, there were hundreds of acres of usable stuff—steel pipe, lumber, tools, tents, Jerry cans, mosquito nets, footlockers, lamps, fridges, bicycles and more. It sounded too good to be true but I found out later that it was true. Along the way, I was to keep an eye out for any additional items I thought we could use. Comfort items.

Barter was important because nothing was free, not even for same-country forces. The professionals I knew in our Force Service Support Group were adept at barter and knew how to drive a good deal. They had made careers at it. Their hands too were tied by the conundrum of needing to keep the *ninety-day pack-up* intact.

I learned that the best barter items for Marine Corps currency were cases or pallets of C-rats, which the Air Force preferred for in-flight meals. I could call The Rose Garden and have pallets of C-rations shipped. We had them and to spare. And brown Navy goatskin flight jackets. Every flier wanted one. Most still do. I hornswoggled our Wing Headquarters on the flight jackets to use as currency. Marine K-Bar knives were highly valued and beer was always welcome. My first deals were struck with men on the C-141s that traded in and out of the Garden bringing mail and people. We could turn in for replacement, or *survey,* gear that was unusable due to wear and tear like flight jackets and K-bars but we could not get into the pack-up. Which was what we really needed.

I headed out first to Tachikawa AFB in Japan on a quest for mattresses. This base was being closed or streamlined. A guy on the USAF C-141 mail bird had told me the U.S. government was paying Japanese nationals two-dollars per mattress to take mattresses out of the barracks and bury them. I put in my order for 100 of those mattresses and saved our government $200. Got them for nothing. In the bargain, I got 100 wooden

170

nightstands free. I learned later the arrival of this materiel at the Garden caused quite a fuss. Men lined up to get their mattresses. Difficulties ensued. Along with the mattresses, I found 1,000 feet of three-inch pipe and 20 barrels of road tar right off the bat. I struck a deal, traded and started these supplies on their way back to the Garden while I went on to the Philippines.

At Clark AFB, I found a bonus—a wrecked blue Air Force jeep that I got for almost nothing. I recalled what our metal shop had done to Clipper's wrecked jeep that infamous night. Once back at the Garden, the jeep was restored, repainted olive drab instead of blue, and driven. It's probably still in the Marine Corps inventory somewhere. There are never enough jeeps. The road tar was put down immediately, the steel pipe laid. Soon The Rose Garden had potable water in new places. I had a lot of fun doing my job and learning another version of how things actually got done in the Marine Corps.

Plus my job got me out of the Garden. By then, the short-timers were counting the days until they rotated out back to the world. Travel distracted me from a lot of that. I was moving. And the job confirmed for me where the Marine Corps was on the Defense Department food chain. The Navy comes close to us in cumshawing—or scrounging—gear but Marines can damn near make a living on what the Army and Air Force throw away.

***

By the time I got back from that first scrounging trip, Rat was leaving us to become operations officer of VMFA-232. The second part of his split tour. The good part. Months later, after I was back in the States, I received a letter from Headquarters, United States Marine Corps, HQMC. Inside the envelope I found a single sheet of notebook paper folded around a crisp new 20-dollar-bill. The pencil-written note said, *"Dear Lt. Lentz, Fuck you. Strong letter to follow."* It was signed Rat. He was good for his word. I kept that letter.

***

When Rat left Group, we were to catch the next poor Heavy coming in as our new boss. Rat told us that his replacement was a tough guy. He had better be. He did not know what was about to hit him.

That's how another major, callsign Razor, became our new boss in April 1973. The day he walked into the S-4 hootch, he was almost in tears. He felt that jolt of betrayal too. He had been promised a gun squadron, not a staff job, but a staff job in Group was what he got. I will never forget the look on that man's face. It was as if someone had hit him between the eyes with a sledge hammer. Shock and disbelief with anger on the side.

Razor said we would start work at the same time tomorrow morning but for now we should take the rest of the day off. Then he left, blue Dutch Master Cigar smoke trailing behind him like a roaring freight train. He headed straight for the thatched-roof Officers Club to drink away his new assignment for the moment. Razor turned out to be a taut, smart, professional man. He had grown up on the streets of Brooklyn and had more common sense than any other officer I ever worked under. He was a pilot who had successfully transitioned from choppers to Phantoms. He had been in Udorn in 1962 when the U.S. was officially not there. Proof of not being there was that his UH-43 chopper, the last piston-powered model flown, had all its U.S. and Marine Corps markings painted over in black.

The Company, or CIA, was surreptitiously resupplying Hmong and other tribal mercenaries, who were our allies. At that time, Marines knew only roughly what was going down. They just followed orders. One day, Razor's mission was to taxi to a location at RTAFB Udorn, await loading, proceed to a set of coordinates on the artillery maps and hover. He heard strange noises and smelled strange smells as his chopper was being loaded. He felt the chopper jerk around. Could have been Hmong warriors that the chopper was transporting, he thought. He got the thumbs up from the loadmaster and lifted off, flew to the coordinates, went into a hover and sat still in the air.

Then the chopper bucked. His crew chief signaled the load was off and Razor turned the chopper around to see what had been dumped. What he saw was a water buffalo spread-eagle in the air, headed straight for the ground. The buffalo hit, dead on impact. Then out of the surrounding jungle, mercenaries with long knives descended on the resupply buffalo. Razor did not stay to watch. But he did not forget either.

**

The day after Razor arrived at The Rose Garden in 1973, he stood us up, said to prepare, to get ready. A Red Rocket warning order could come at any time to activate Operation Sunset, which would mean the end of the war for us at The Rose Garden. The longer we had to get ready, the better it would be. I laughed to myself, thinking of the bet that Rat had made me that the retrograde wouldn't come on my watch. Yeah, right. He wasn't given the callsign Rat without a reason.

172

Chapter 33. Squadron to Group

In the meantime, Razor sort of adopted me. He saw something in me that he thought should stay in the Marine Corps. He tried to teach me all the officer-and-gentleman skills he thought I'd need to know in a Marine Corps career—how to play Bridge, groom superiors in the best non-kiss-ass way, play golf, buy jewelry for a wife, send thank you notes, select the right wines. And how to compete at anything. And win.

I didn't see myself being a career Marine officer, didn't want to see it. I still planned to do my contractual time and leave the Corps behind. For most of my life, I had heard stories about men who could not hack it outside of a government job. My father had a jaundiced view of that way of life, so I had issues with making the Marines my career. Plus my father's learned dictum always burned in the back of my mind—*He who lives by the sword, dies by the sword.* I did not want to die by the sword. And we were still in war. It could still only take one bad hop to ruin your whole day.

But Razor didn't give up on me. Knowing what we would have to face in the next few weeks, he sent me to an Air Force Load Commander Embarkation school short course in Okinawa so that I could understand how C-141s and C-5s were loaded. I also studied ships loading characteristics pamphlets, SLCPs, and learned about the ships that would carry our gear that couldn't fit on C-5s, the biggest cargo planes that existed at the time.

We had templates drawn of what gear would go where on the ships we'd been told we could expect to use for the retrograde. We made it all fit on paper. That information turned out to be dead wrong but I became intimate with the loading decks, cargo nets, king-post capacities, holds and tonnages available for what we were going to have to move.

During this time, I stayed on the asses of the embarkation people in the different units. I knew most of the responsible people in the units and made sure they updated me on changes in tonnage, requirements and configurations. Their weekly reporting provided real data so that when the retrograde order came, we would know actually what it would take to get us out.

Most embarkation officers, both Group and grunt, were good. One grunt embark officer even went on to become the highest-ranking man in the United States military—Captain Pete Pace. He later served as Chairman of the Joint Chief of Staff under President George W. Bush. Pete Pace was the first Marine to hold that position. When he did, the entire U.S. Marine Corps received a promotion. But not everyone I dealt with was as forthcoming as Pete Pace—or the caliber man he was.

The distinction between billet and rank was often a friction point. There was a lot of push and shove during the retrograde and I had the billet or assigned job that required both. Yet the Marine Corps' stubborn empha-sis on rank caused some officers who out-ranked me to resent a lower-grade officer like me calling the shots and giving orders.

I had a near-miss fistfight with one recalcitrant unit embark. My ad-versary was a Mustang RIO, a captain from VMFA-232, who simply wanted to kick my ass. He probably could have since he had been an all–Southwest Conference linebacker at Texas A&M in the pre-coed days. Though I was only a first lieutenant in rank and he was a captain, I was his senior since I worked for the Group, a higher echelon of command and control than a squadron, so my position carried authority over his. This embark officer flat out disobeyed my order to move some of his materiel so a repair crew could get in to fix a C-5 that had broken down and was gumming everything up.

"I don't take orders from a wise-ass punk first lieutenant," he responded. "My Marine Corps doesn't work that way."

I shouted that I didn't give a damn about the Marine Corps bullshit he was talking about. "I want that stuff moved," I told him. "You don't have a choice. This isn't a request."

My adversary tried a threat. "How would you like me to write you up for insubordination? Or disrespect of a senior officer." I remembered what I had learned early at The Rose Garden. Rank among company-grade officers was like virtue among prostitutes.

"Do whatever the hell you want," I said, "but get that shit moved!" I knew that I could not back away. Empty planes were on the way in and stick line space was at a premium.

He fired back, "Bub, you say one more word to me and I will knock your block off."

I just stood there because I saw Captain Agile taking all this in. Agile had a puzzled smile on his face. He too was a stout ECP, holding the same rank as my adversary but in the higher echelon Group. He too was a hard-nosed hard-ass. But lucky for me, he was *my* hard-ass.

Agile walked up and said, "Hey, you. *I* am senior to you by billet. You are using rank to cover up your screw-up. Since you are playing hard guy, listen to this. I am giving you a legal and lawful order right now to clear out of Lieutenant Lentz's face. And if you don't get your shit moved, *I* will write *you* up. Then we will go see the Colonel together—in about five minutes. Your call."

The embark officer glowered knowing he had been trumped. He looked at me and said, "I'll see *you* later."

Agile looked the testy unit embark officer in the eye. "No, you'll see *us*

Chapter 33. Squadron to Group

later. Lieutenant Lentz is just doing his job and his job is a hell of a lot bigger than your job." That ended that.

I thanked Agile. "This guy is a very big prima donna," he said. "People don't stand up to him."

When we saw Razor later, we told him about the confrontation. His reaction was, "Fuck him and the horse he rode in on. We have too much to do to put up with that shit."

CHAPTER 34

Operation Sunset

August–September 1973

The order to activate Operation Sunset came in August 1973. I remember waking up to Razor telling us the retrograde was on and the first C-141 was due in that afternoon. I had been doing all I could to get supplies in and now I had to use all I knew to start shipping everything out. The word went out to all the unit commanders and I met with my squadron counterparts. Each knew where to place his *sticks*, rows of loaded, strapped-down pallets of cargo, and their rolling stock of ground support gear and jeeps, all with emptied gas tanks.

From that day on, it was to be C-141s and C-130s and an occasional C-5, nose to tail, or, as military folk like to say, asshole to bellybutton, until we were done. We used 98 C-141 loads, 13 C-5 loads and way too many C-130 loads to count. Start to finish, the process took 23 days, carried off without mishap.

Some gear like our one P&H crane was too tall and heavy for even a C-5 to carry. Outsized gear like that left The Rose Garden by truck. An Inter-Service Support Agreement, ISSA, had to be cut for military contract trucking, which would all be done by Thai civilians. During the war, an ISSA form would have been used for things like delivery of ice and burning the waste from the heads but now an ISSA was being used to take a crane 300 miles down to Samae San, the U.S. Army Port near Bangkok, to wait for a ship. I just thought it odd that the Army had its own port. I lost count of how many flatbed trucks hauled away equipment.

Throughout this process, The Rose Garden proper began to feel eerie. Its population eventually dwindled to about 50 men. As the move-out went on, the few facilities we had were shut down little by little. The people who remained on base moved into empty hootches and ate out of C-rat cans. Baths became fewer and fewer and then stopped altogether. The body odor got pretty rank since during that month the temperature was near 100 degrees Fahrenheit every day.

Chapter 34. Operation Sunset

Things were ending but we carried on. Right about then, we finally named the little streets around the base after the Garden's Marine flyers who had gone down. The tin-benders made real street signs mounted on poles. Chipman Street, Cordova Street, Forrester Street, Kroboth Street, Peacock Street, Price Street, Robertson Street. Al Kroboth was the only one of these downed flyers who made it back alive. At the same time, some of the indigenous Thai people erected a crude sign with stars and stripes that said in English *Don't Leave. We Want You to Stay.*

After the last of the unit's gear had been loaded and flown out, a quiet fell. The night jungle was louder than any of us could remember. Frogs, crickets, large insects and monkeys once again became audible. Three days later Razor, Agile and I left Nam Phong for Bangkok, among the last men out. Razor already had his next duty assignment. He was to take over as executive officer of a fighter squadron, a job he cherished, a job he knew was an essential step for him to get what he wanted most—general's rank and his own flag. Agile was a career man as well and had his next transfer in hand to the same squadron where Razor was going. For a young-ish captain in the Marine Corps, he was in good shape. Not long after Agile joined that squadron, Razor moved up from XO to CO.

That left me isolated in the isolation. I had a life to go back to. I still planned to get out of the Marine Corps. I had little more than two years of obligated time left once I reported post–Vietnam to Austin, Texas. After that, I did not have a plan much less a career. I had just spent the worst and best year of my life but that year had not moved me in any specific career direction. It had just been a year in the war of my time, a year that had altered my life. I had only a foggy notion of how much.

I look at the photographs of me in those days and wonder who that guy in the pictures is. No young man or woman will come away unchanged after a year of actual, sometimes immediate, life-or-death situations, with responsibilities for the lives of other people. That kind of reality can take a person from age 27 to age 70 in about five minutes.

For three days there was time, unwanted time, to think about all of that, to feel grief, nostalgia, uncertainty. Nam Phong was the last place that some men I had known and cared about saw in life. That had to count for something but what? We were leaving and if the Thai nation didn't reclaim the base, the jungle would.

In those days of unwanted time, I started making lists just as I had on my arriving flight to The Rose Garden. Mentally I listed what had been, what had been given up, what had been lost. The list of things lost started with men, young like I was. Near the top of that list of men was a young Marine who left behind an infant son to grow up without ever knowing his father. I vowed to track down that surviving son, to sit with him, if he wanted, but I haven't done that yet. That son would be close to 50 by now.

***

Once out of The Rose Garden and in proximity to Bangkok, we began to move back to civilization, to decompress. Razor tried to teach me to play golf at the U–Tapao Royal Thai Air Force Base Golf Course. We had several pretty good meals by Thai standards and we had the luxury of being able to clean ourselves up.

Razor and I headed separately to Iwakuni, Japan. He would sign for whatever gear from the Garden was destined for Japan and I was re-attached to Group rear in garrison, not deployed in war. I would be back in the world in a week or so.

I hooked up with Razor once while we were in Japan. He continued to try to teach me golf. He tried to snivel a bird one day so we could fly a hop together but it didn't happen.

That week the first military sealift command ship, MSCS, used to float out our gear had docked in Japan. We learned that not one strand of copper wire on any of the machines we had marshaled had survived being loaded out. Generators and electrical motors of all sizes arrived completely stripped. That materiel had been left under the guardianship of the Thai Army. Letters signed by various Thai officials stated as much. Razor and I went to Wing Headquarters and gave depositions as to what had happened and how. No Task Force Delta support was to be found.

By then, I had only a few days left in Wes-Pac. I'd taken the money I'd saved and bought the requisite stereo tape deck at the PX. I received my port call and knew when to meet my freedom bird. Razor was with me when I got on. It was difficult not to be emotional but somehow we stayed dry-eyed and promised to keep in touch.

A day later I got back to Travis AFB, Fairfield, California, the same place I had left roughly one year earlier. I had about ten hours to get to San Francisco International Airport, SFO, for my flight to Texas. We had all heard arrival stories. Walking in uniform at SFO, I saw a group of what we then called third-world women. American women with hairy legs and hairier armpits. They came towards me. I could feel their eyes on me but I kept my pace and listened without hearing as they passed. I thought one of them spat at me but if she did, she missed.

Chapter 34. Operation Sunset

Once safe and dry on my Delta flight to Texas, I was treated to extra drinks and all the sandwiches I could eat. The flight attendants were very nice and outwardly appreciative. I arrived in Waco and tried to become re-acquainted with my wife. Two weeks later, we moved to Austin and I re-started my Marine Corps life post–Rose Garden and *sans* Phantoms.

***

In Austin, I was an officer selection officer, OSO. I had been assigned an officer recruiting position, which I thought would be my last active duty job with the Marines. While I was there, I received a letter from Razor, now the CO of VMFA-232, the squadron he'd always wanted. He invited me to his change of command ceremony in the Philippines. I was knocked over. Of course, I could not make it but the thought was there.

Near the bottom of the official letter was a handwritten note—*"Fleet, I would never have gotten here without you."* One of the greatest compliments I ever received as a Marine. I have the letter still.

In August 1974, I was able to see Razor in Washington, D.C., when I was ordered up to HQMC charm school for OSOs. He had taken a job that would get him deep selected for colonel—considered for early promotion ahead of the promotion zone of his peers.

We had a blast. Razor was wearing the civilian clothes that the Department of Defense, Washington, required on certain days. The government was careful that Washington didn't appear as an armed camp. When I left, Razor was smiling. He told me he would nail colonel. He knew how to do it. That was the last time I would see him.

***

By the late seventies, I had left the flying Marine Corps altogether. I had done a year of flying based out of Dallas but my heart wasn't in it. Post-Vietnam, the remaining airplanes were old and falling apart. As a result, we lost some aircrew and planes that we should not have. Even back from The Rose Garden, I still had an aversion to the idea of living and dying by the sword.

I thought I had quit flying for good. I was working a civilian job in the Lower Rio Grande Valley, trying to find a way to go home again. One morning in 1980, I heard on the radio that a mid-air collision had occurred off the coast of Beaufort, South Carolina. I knew it had to be Marines.

I called Dallas and talked to some of the Marine F-4 guys I knew who were still flying. Razor had been piloting one of the two F-4s that collided that night, almost nose to nose, at supersonic speeds. In his back seat had been another Rose Garden veteran and salt, callsign Suitcase, a friend as well. But there was not and never will be another friend like Razor.

It must have been a spectacularly grim collision—a flick of orange lightning, a massive booming thunder clap and then the sound of pieces of metal dropping into the silent ocean. No remains were ever found.

Razor's death struck me as few others had. I left work and drove around with no destination in mind. I reviewed everything I could remember that ever passed between us. I had a clear memory of his face that hauntingly, metaphysically, came back as a way for him to check-in with me. I could clearly hear him railing at me—

You stopped flying, Fleet? For God's sake why? Well, at least you kept your commission.

Looks to me like you're not doing so red hot, pal. You'd better pull your act together and go do something you are half decent at doing.

You tell me you don't want to fly anymore? I tell you, do not bullshit me.

Now get your ass back into the cockpit while you still can. I gave you the keys to the kingdom, my best shots, my best moves. You are supposed to keep it going. I invested in you! Don't play me.

Now enough of the civilian bit. You're terrible at it. Get back into the Phantom as soon as you can.

I heard him. I listened to him. And because he thought I should, I went back to Marine Corps flying. Only a few months later, I graduated from Navy Fighter Weapons School, aka Top Gun. On that day, with a nod upward to Razor, I toasted him with a Tanqueray and tonic. The proper drink according to him. Not too many, not too few.

I was able to fly long enough to earn 20 good years and a retirement. Along the way I was given command of a Marine Aviation Logistics Squadron, MALS-41, after serving as executive officer of a gun squadron, VMFA-112, in Dallas. Later, I was promoted again and retired with the rank of colonel.

I never really stopped flying. And Razor was right, that was good for me.

SECTION FIVE

Takeaways

CHAPTER 35

Takeaways

2020

Start with today, I'm now 74. Several men I flew with and served with, officer and enlisted, are still close friends. Routinely, I hear from them and communicate with them. We do not do rose-colored looks back down memory lane. All of us are too cold-eyed for that. We lived and flew together out of an aviation environment that smelled like jet fuel and shit. And we survived. I value those friendships from that year in Vietnam as I do no others. I am the richer for them. Those friendships are the most valuable keepers from my days in The Rose Garden. They are braided into my life.

***

From the point of view of a Marine officer, The Rose Garden was an invaluable experience. I was actually a part of what the expeditionary Marine Corps was established to do—deploy, set up and enter combat with scarce resources. To me, that remains the hallmark of being a Marine. We can be sent anywhere at any time, under strange conditions, then be expected to perform. I lived this life for a year and saw how *expeditionary* was done.

When I became a squadron commander in 1989, I did my best to instill that ethic into the members of my squadron. The squadron had volunteered to go to Desert Storm. Even though we were not selected to go, we were prepared to be expeditionary Marines.

***

Clipper was my template for a squadron commander. My takeaway from him in that role was to keep my unit in the best shape possible mentally and physically. There was more to that than meets the eye. He told me once that *being a squadron commander is like when your mother told you to act like you've been there before. Then you'd better get to the paperwork and learn what the hell is actually going on.* On his first command, he acted like

183

he'd been a squadron commander before, based on the models of the men he had served under. I did the same.

Clipper had command presence—call it charisma—to spare. Everyone in the squadron knew he was the leader and would follow him. Mostly because he led from the front, was smart, wasn't afraid of anything and found the humor in the most miserable conditions. I wanted to be that way. But Clipper could also occasionally behave like a second lieutenant. He behaved this way, in part, to be entirely accessible to his men. He always kept his men's interest at heart.

I also learned from him to act as a shield to keep needless make-work from landing on my folks. I went to bat for them if they were treated unfairly by the system. Cut through the mickey mouse.

Thirty-five years after the war, Clipper organized a gathering of The Rose Garden Silver Eagles. Just us. Clipper taught us never to forget what we had done together and we learned that lesson well. He had told us when we were in the pits of the Garden that those days *were* the good old days. We knew that he had real affection for us, which is difficult for a bunch of hard-charging young men to accept. He communicated that affection with élan. We all felt a strange, twisted bond.

***

When I became a colonel in 1991, I turned to the template for leadership laid down by the Joker years earlier in The Rose Garden. Joker was the colonel I knew best under combat conditions. Joker had five squadrons under his command—three gun squadrons, HAMS and MABS—and three detachments—choppers, tankers, and a security battalion. He handled well many diverse and pressing responsibilities under demanding circumstances.

From him, I learned basic humility. As the CO of MAG-15 he never pulled rank. He did not demand special treatment or deference because of his rank alone. But he could have. Later, I saw many other colonels who did pull rank for lesser reasons. Joker ate with us, lived in a hootch as we did and flew with us.

He did what was necessary to care for his men, whatever the cost, whether that action bent rules or not. I witnessed from him the power of the strength of conviction. It is my belief that the decision he made late in the war to limit our hops to only one run at a target may have cost him. It circulated through The Rose Garden grapevine that when Joker changed the Rules of Engagement, he said *"Not any truck in Laos was worth one of my planes or aircrews."* That comment brought sighs of relief to many, including me. During my years as a colonel, I thought of him often. He epitomized awareness and concern for his men, turned into action.

***

The enlisted men and senior staff at The Rose Garden taught me how to get jobs done under trying conditions. Those men are too numerous to mention. *Mea culpa*. They served as stalwart examples. Many will never know that I learned from them how to be a decent and effective officer.

***

During all of my 20-odd flying years, I had the He Coon, Suitcase, Square, Maggot, the Fat Maggot, and many others sitting in the cockpit with me. They had taught me tricks to keep the planes safely in the air. But there is nothing like going through an emergency yourself and surviving it to test those tricks, to etch in the lessons learned.

Besides the tricks that I learned from my fellow Marine aviators, I learned that the way of being and acting in the cockpit is as important as anything. Calmness under duress, keeping things steady and workable. There is always something positive that can be tried until your last option— to eject. Years after the war when I was in the aviation business, I would often casually remark *at least nobody is shooting at us*. Sometimes that wry remark worked to helped ameliorate the bad situation. It often works for me to this very day.

***

I learned to break big words like courage into smaller pieces based on what I had seen and experienced. I learned that courage, even courage in war, has many different faces. The most notable examples of courage were the prisoners of war, two of whom I knew personally: Jim Walsh and Al Kroboth. Both men were Marines. They both were kept in the infamous tiger cages, survived torture, resisted and persevered. Having nothing to fight back with, Jim would defecate in his hand and throw the feces at his captors when they came near enough to be hit. His resistance has been in-cluded in the *Guidebook for Marines* as an example of what could be done to resist. When Al was shot down, his body was broken in several places and he had no medical attention. Then he was forced to walk from South to North Vietnam.

A friend of mine in the Silver Eagles demonstrated a different kind of courage, a more personal kind. The courage of listening to his inner guide, following the strength of his convictions and staying loyal. He quickly realized that the odds were stacked against him for surviving The Rose Garden and questioned the worth of hanging in until the end of the war, possibly dying early for the sake of knocking out trucks on roads in Laos. He took a set of orders that sent him to Okinawa as an FAC with the grunts. But he chose to return to The Rose Garden. When I asked him why, he responded, "I couldn't leave you assholes here without me." He served out this tour, flew several more combat hops and rotated back to the world. His example of courage may seem to contradict the persistent professionalism of others, like Ducks. But somehow, I know both examples to be true.

***

I learned the importance of the ability to make fast decisions in dire circumstances and then to live with my decisions. To trust my instincts. But I also learned to listen, when I could, to my colleagues before making a big decision that would affect us all. To read the situation and analyze what kind of support my decision would have. To always have a plan, then a plan B and sometimes a plan C.

I learned to tell the truth, as best I knew it, to myself and to those I was working with. To be true to myself. Though we had no ready room at The Rose Garden, the ready-room atmosphere permeated our de-briefs wherever they took place and taught me this lesson. The ready room was no place for bullshit. It was a place where the truth came out, stories were picked apart, and holes were shot into misinterpretations or misrepresentations.

Epilogue:
Going Back

December 2000

I returned as a civilian to Vietnam, to Hanoi and Saigon, in 1997, then again in 2000. A number of things took me back—a series of circumstances involving civilian aviation business and a friendship with a U.S. Senator tied to the fact that I still held rank in the Marine reserves. I was traveling with others but I was the only one of our entourage who had served in the war.

As I expected, that visit, that return, was permeated with strangeness. I was determined to be open to it, to let my return tell me whatever it had to tell me, to let it just unfold as it came rather than inspect it through the lens of what others might expect.

In 1997, relations between the U.S. and Vietnam were still somewhat raw and ambiguous, but improving. I knew there was no guarantee of the reception I'd get. It had become common for American men to return to Vietnam to try to piece together what had happened there. What it all meant. But I had avoided listening too much about any of these experiences because I wanted my return to be wholly my own.

This time, I was just a passenger flying comfortably from Saigon to Hanoi on an Air Vietnam Boeing airliner. As we boarded the plane at the Ton Sohn Nhut airport in Saigon, a Vietnamese man I was talking with about the war made an idle remark about the difference between American-built infrastructure and the infrastructure at the Gia Lam Airport, which is what the Russians had left. "All shit," he said, "All shit. Not American, no. American very good. Russian, all shit." When we landed there, I saw what he meant.

Looking out of the window of the plane, I could still clearly pick out Da Nang's parallel runways. I saluted my friend Mr. Tones and remembered our flight to Cubi Point when the runways were our sight marker. I located Quang Tri and Hue so I had a good idea of where we were. Like a good

Epilogue

RIO, I was still navigating. I started to feel myself tighten up as we began descending into Hanoi. We were landing just outside the city. I had never seen Gia Lam but I had often heard its name broadcast over the air as a site where SAMs were being launched.

We landed and rolled out. It was the bumpiest, roughest landing I had ever felt. I was on edge and weary from a combination of travel and apprehension. There was no jetway to walk down, only a decrepit air stair. The Gia Lam area of Hanoi was like the American Wild West without the horses. The sidewalks were raised wooden planks over the red soil. Everything was done by hand and on foot.

It was night when our group caught a one-eyed taxi into the city. The driver took us down a dark dirt road that cut across several farmyards. It was a head-trip driving through an area that had once housed a MiG base. Had I not a specific job to do, the trip would have been even more mind warping. Flying and riding comfortably over weirdly hallowed ground, I realized it would be difficult to relate to the others what was going on inside me. After an hour in this taxi, my traveling party arrived at a rundown Vietnamese hotel. I drank enough to loosen that strung-out feeling. I drank enough to help me sleep.

The next day, another member of our party and I took another cab to a rented building that was serving as the U.S. Embassy. Part of our task was to deliver an official government document to the then-serving U.S. Ambassador in Hanoi, the Honorable Pete Peterson, a former Air Force pilot who had been a POW for six years. Pulling up in front of the embassy—a modest rented 1960s office building—I saw a sooty gray American flag hanging limply on a flagpole. Unexpectedly, I began weeping quietly. My companion on this assignment—a rough and tumble outdoorsman, a pilot, former Marine and entrepreneur from Montana—gestured to the driver to wait a minute.

Whatever it was that hit me passed. I composed myself and we walked into the Embassy. A red carpet, as dirty as the flag, had been rolled out and a U.S. Marine sergeant attached to the embassy came to attention and gave a hand salute. Like all U.S. embassies, this one was guarded by Marines. The sergeant said, "A good day to you, sirs. This is our first day to stand the duty. We were officially installed just this morning. We heard there was a Marine officer with you. Welcome aboard, sir." I returned the salute even though it wasn't proper to do so since I wasn't in uniform. I shook the sergeant's hand, hoping like hell my tears had not left tracks. It didn't really matter though. The tears came for their own reasons. I was not ashamed of them.

Going Back

In the Ambassador's office, we introduced ourselves. Ambassador Peterson was cordial and we delivered the document entrusted to us. After some chitchat, he invited us to his back office that was located behind the official one. Once the doors had closed, he broke out a bottle of bourbon and we toasted. My mind was fixed on what I wanted to say to him. I wanted to apologize for not being able to get him and the other POWs out in 1972 and I did. And then I asked, "With all due respect to your rank, sir, why in the hell would you want to come back here?"

He smiled just a little. "Mainly I came back to oversee the search for the remains of the missing American flyers. I knew a lot of them, some because I flew with them, some because I met them when I was a POW at Ho Lao. I wanted them found. I wanted them identified and their remains returned home. And I had another reason. I came back because I thought coming back would help me get past it."

Hearing his answer, I vowed then and there that if he could come back and deal with everything, after all he'd been through, I sure as hell could work harder on getting past it too. He had survived brutal imprisonment—my worst nightmare of war—and he was thriving.

Our group left the Embassy and was driven to the old Metropole Hotel, which looked like paradise to me after all the dirt roads and the rundown hotel from the night before. The thick soot of soft coal dust clung to us and we could see it in the air but this hotel's French Colonial architecture with its recent paint job was sparkling white in the airy sea of gray soft-coal-burned haze. It was near Christmas and as we walked inside, we saw the hotel staff standing in the lobby around a huge real Christmas tree. They were singing carols and that brought another quick wash of tears. It seemed to be a time of tears.

The next day, we found ourselves with time on our hands. One of my companions and I went on a tour of Hanoi town. A war museum was crammed with downed American airplanes and an American tank along with many big guns and small arms that captured American soldiers had carried. Along the walls were black and white photographic panels of utterly dejected POWs shuffling along in chains.

Mounted on stands were the museum's prize displays, the actual MiGs that had been flown by their leading aces. I thought it odd that they memorialized the machines of war while we memorialized the men who fought, making them heroes. Sometimes. We saw a photograph of the lake John McCain parachuted into after being hit, just before his capture.

Near midnight, I walked alone to the Hanoi Hilton, Ho Lao prison,

189

Epilogue

Enemy fighter MiG-15 in the Air Museum, Hanoi, North Vietnam. The photograph was taken by the author during his trip back to Vietnam in 2000. The museum was crammed with MiGs that had been flown by North Vietnam's leading aces along with many downed American airplanes, guns and small arms (author's collection).

where so many of our men had died as prisoners of war after enduring hell on earth. I had come to pay my respects in the dark and silence. Entering what had been such a fearsome place, I found it ironic that Hanoi was very safe to walk in now that the war was over. Strict law had soaked way down into the society. After I returned to the hotel, I took a scalding hot shower and hit my rack. By the time I was in bed, it was nearly two o'clock in the morning and I didn't want to feel anything anymore.

I awoke early the next day and walked into the outdoor restaurant in courtyard gardens in the center of the hotel. The sun was not quite up and I was the first to arrive for breakfast. I took a seat at an elegantly laid out table and a young lady of indecipherable age, wearing the traditional white Vietnamese *ao dai*, quietly walked over. She smiled demurely and asked if I would like coffee. I told her I wanted a whole pot and when she realized I wasn't joking, she brought over a full steaming silver pot and a Beleek fine china cup. She handed me a menu and bowed slightly as she turned away.

The morning light was slowly beginning to rise along the vines covering the wall of the garden. I could make out the darts of swallows swooping high in the sky above where I was sitting. The track I had flown 25 years earlier was not very far southwest from the linen-covered table where I was now having very good Vietnamese coffee. Twenty-five years earlier, we had wanted, intended, to bomb this place flat. Sitting there I couldn't sort out my feelings. I couldn't connect the past and the present. Then, now, then, now. All the same life. Damn.

The young lady returned to take my order. Three scrambled eggs, bacon, ham, a stack of toast with butter and a small jar of orange marmalade. As she turned to leave, I politely stopped her. "Would you mind if I ask you some questions?" She halted, smiling again, and said no, she would not.

I told her that I knew it was not good manners to ask a woman her age but I would like to know hers. I wanted to see if she was of the age of the war time. She said she would turn 25 in January, the following month. She was being carried by her mother when we were bombing. She was born in Hanoi.

I had to tell her why I wanted to know and I struggled to find a civilized way of doing it. "I was here," I said, "thirty miles from here, there." I pointed through the swallows. Then I said the only thing I could find to say, "I am so glad we did not kill your parents." And then I couldn't say anymore. My throat constricted and my eyes watered.

She said, "It was not your fault. It was your government and my government. Now we are glad you are here." The look on her face never changed. It was neither smiling nor severe. "I will bring you your breakfast. You are hungry," she said and her sweet smile returned.

Later, my companion and I rented a bicycle-powered rickshaw. We played around with the driver, getting him to sit as a passenger while we took turns cycling for a while. This amused not only the driver but also the Vietnamese we passed by.

That afternoon, my traveling companion gave a scheduled goodwill speech to some local dignitaries, including the officers of the Vietnamese equivalent of our Federal Aviation Administration. The chief's name was Nguyen Hong Nhi and we were told that he had been North Vietnam's leading ace during the war. I was not about to question his claim to 12.5 kills in the war, not then and there.

Beyond comporting himself as a fighter pilot, Mr. Nguyen came across as an alpha predator, all five-feet six-inches of him. He had the eyes of one. Meeting him I was thrown into an internal conflict that I held down tightly. I was at a loss as to how to countenance this man. I had no proof that there was a dossier on me that he might have seen before my arrival but I had

Epilogue

been told that the North had information on all of us who flew. We had even gone to lengths of filing secret code words at our headquarters intelligence section to be used for positive identification had we gone down and needed rescuing.

Mr. Nguyen may have known that at one time I would have gladly blown his airplane out from around him, just as he would have done to mine. As far as I know, that was my first and only handshake with a former declared enemy. I admit to liking the small rush I got from towering over the little man but my superior height did not take one thing away from what he was purported to have done. He was good. In a professional sense, I had to respect his accomplishments but I did so with as little enthusiasm as I could muster. His demeanor never changed. He was entirely focused on what the interpreter said to him. He stayed dead serious.

Over the next few years, his agency and my company shared in a couple of mutually beneficial business transactions. Whether any or all of them could be traced directly to that afternoon, I cannot say. I followed his business career through various aviation trade publications. He did a good job for his country in his administrative position and retired peacefully.

***

Just a few years ago in Reno, Nevada, I attended the one and only VMFA-115 Silver Eagles reunion since the war. The reunion Clipper had organized. I didn't mention that I had met Mr. Nguyen. I didn't bring up that I had gone back. I didn't relive much except with Nacho about Angkor Wat. I woke up the morning after the first night of that reunion feeling more peaceful than I had felt in many years.

I remembered Ambassador Pete Peterson, former POW, and was glad he'd lived through the war, glad I met him, glad I'd been able to keep the promise I made to myself when I did.

Except for five or six, every man I had learned to care about who had survived the war was at the reunion. We had phone numbers for the ones who hadn't been able to make it. We called them up late at night and gave them some friendly shit. It was a way of saying *We miss you*. It wasn't bad. Not bad at all.

Appendix A:
Map of Vietnam and
Neighboring Countries

Map of Vietnam and neighboring countries.

Appendix B:
Glossary of Terms

The following explanations are written to assist a non-military reader of this book. Official military explanations would be much more detailed and sometimes very technical.

Ace   An aircrew that has shot down at least five enemy aircraft in combat

Air Defense Identification Zone, **ADIZ**   A line drawn around a country on a map, forming an air border that requires permission to cross

Air Liaison Officer, ALO   An aviation officer assigned to work with Infantry

Air Medal   An award based on meritorious performance over a period of time and intensity, usually in aerial combat. A single mission air medal is awarded for a particular flight that displayed achievement, and is senior to an Air Medal.

Air Order of Battle   Enemy defenses that increased in intensity, as a fighter plane approached a target. Developed from intelligence and experience to inform fighters of what to expect on a combat hop.

Airborne Command and Control, **ACC** Airborne command post routing friendly aircraft to a target and on-scene commanders or Forward Air Controllers

All Officers Meeting, **AOM**   Meeting ordered by the commanding officer

Always check your six   *Protect your rear in the air,* using clock code. The nose of the airplane is always twelve o'clock.

Glossary of Terms

***Anti-aircraft artillery,* AAA**   Triple-A fire Light- to heavy-caliber forward-firing guns capable of extreme range and destruction

Armstrong   Missiles armed

Basketball   Callsign for KC-130 aircraft used for refueling by VMFA-115

***Big Ugly Fat Fucker, Big Ugly Fat Fellow,* BUFF, B-52**   Old, heavy bombers developed during the Cold War

Billet   A place to stay or an ordered job assignment

Bingoed   Left a position with enough fuel to get home

Bird Colonel   Full colonel, pay grade 0–6, as opposed to Lieutenant Colonel, pay grade 0–5

Black Ferraris   Black boots, jungle or flight

Bogey   Radar presentation of unknown cause, perhaps an enemy aircraft

***Bomb Damage Assessment,* BDA**   Percent effectiveness of the target hit and destroyed, a score given by the Forward Air Controller, FAC, on scene

Boola-boola   Fighter slang for a drone being blown up during a peace-time missile firing exercise

Brief, debrief, rebrief   Brief—usually lasting an hour covering pertinent information on an upcoming mission; debrief—meeting after the mission to go over results and lessons learned; rebrief—in the event of a fast turn-around hop as in returning to The Rose Garden, a quick brief.

Bull's Eye   Code name for Hanoi

Buster   In full afterburner, at maximum engine speed

C-141   Workhorse cargo plane of the USAF

C-5   A bigger workhorse, fewer in number than the 141s

Callsign   Shorthand designator for a person, squadron, organization, etc.

CAP   Combat Air Patrol, a Section of two planes flying in a race-track holding pattern

Chaff bundle   Aluminum strips shot out of the F-4 to confuse enemy radar

Charlie   The Viet Cong

Cleared hot   Clearance to deliver ordnance

***Commanding Officer*, CO**   Senior man in the squadron, the boss, the skipper

Commissioned Officer   Usually a college graduate who has been through an officer training program and been commissioned on paper by the President of the United States

Contact   What a RIO says when he sees on radar the bogey he is looking for.

Cover   Hat or cap

C-rations   Boxed or canned cold food, much of it decades old, C-rats for short

Daisy cutters   An anti-personnel 500-pound bomb with a 36" fuse extender. Goes off at waist level.

Early-early   A 3:00 a.m. wake-up for a 5:30 a.m. launch

***Emissions Controlled*, Emcon**   Flying status with no radio, no radar, no lights

Enlisted   All ranks below commissioned or warrant officers

***Enlisted Commissioning Program*, ECP**   A program which allowed highly qualified enlisted Marines without a college degree to apply for Officer Candidate School

***Executive Officer*, XO**   Number 2 man in the squadron, reports to the CO

Expeditionary   Sent with short notice to who-knows-where for indefinite periods of time with no immediate resupply

Field Grade Officer   Major, lieutenant colonel, full colonel

Flak trap   A set-up where a plane might be drawn into an enemy trap under misleading circumstances

FNG   Generally understood three-letter identifier standing for *fucking new guy*. Often pejorative or excusatory.

Glossary of Terms

Force Service Support Group, FSSG   A branch of the USMC specializing in maintaining the supply flow of almost all necessities for sustaining a force of size

Forward Air Controller, FAC   On-scene commander on a combat mission

Go/no-go   A point of commitment on a long flight to either proceed or return to land

Group rear in garrison   Group no longer stationed in combat

Grunts   Infantry

Gunnery sergeant   Senior enlisted rank, pay grade E-7, commonly referred to as a gunny; the backbone of the USMC

Hairy buffalo   Marine slang for going to bed without changing clothes or showering

HAMS   Headquarters and Maintenance Squadron

Hardtack   Fried, canned bread or crackers

Heavies   Commissioned officers, majors and above

Hop/test hop/combat hop   A takeoff and landing

Hot-mic/Cold-mic   Hot-mic is instantaneous communication between the two F-4 cockpits; Cold-mic required use of an internal foot-switch for communication between the cockpits.

HQMC   Headquarters Marine Corps

Infantry   Marine ground forces trained to locate, close with and destroy the enemy by fire and maneuver, or repel the enemy's assault by fire and close combat

Intercept   An air-to-air mission to identify a bogey and/or shoot it down

Inter-Cockpit System, ICS   Communication system allowing hot-mic or cold-mic communication between F-4 cockpits

Jerry cans   Five-gallon metal cans used to carry water or fuel

Jink   Violently evade while airborne to avoid being hit

Judy   What the RIO says when he has locked up the bogey with his radar and is in control of the flight

Junior officers   First lieutenants, second lieutenants and captains

KC-130   Propeller-driven cargo aircraft that could be configured to provide aerial refueling

Killed by air, **KBA**   Identified enemy casualties, usually a count

Knife edge   Rolling the F-4 so that the wing tip is perpendicular to the horizon and holding the position briefly

Leave   A recorded requested absence for more than three days

Liberty   Unrequested time off for about three days

Line squadron   A squadron that can be deployed

Lineal number   A number assigned in a document by HQMC, designating who is senior and junior to every officer of his same rank

LORAN   Long-range aid to navigation. Navigation system used by the USAF that allowed a plane to see the target through thick overcast by means of geographical coordinates.

Marine Air Base Squadron, **MABS, MABSters**   A separate squadron responsible for the runway, the crash crew, the fuel farm, a cherry picker retrieval crane and explosive ordnance disposal, among other things

Mark call   Spoken call by the F-4 RIO telling the pilot to release bombs

MCAS   Marine Corps Air Station

MiG   Enemy aircraft; Russian- and Chinese-built fighter aircraft flown by the North Vietnamese Air Force

Military occupational specialty, **MOS**   A number assigned by HQMC to designate what a Marine is formally trained to do

MPC   Military payment currency, also called scrip, funny money

Mustangs   Former enlisted men who have earned commissions

Naval Aviation Training Operations Standardization manual, **NATOPS**   Owner's manual for any aircraft, detailing how it works, what it can and cannot do when airborne

NCO   Noncommissioned officer, an enlisted rank beginning at corporal, E-4, going up to Sgt. Major, E-9

No joy   Code talk for *I do not see or hear what you told me I should see or hear*

Observation   A position in aerial refueling, 1000 feet above or below a KC-130 tanker and 1000 feet off to either side

Officer Selection Officer, **OSO**   One whose task it is to recruit Marine officers

Operations officer   Third-most senior officer in a squadron responsible for daily flight operations; often writes the flight schedule

Pickle Pull   On a bombing hop, when bombs are dropped and the nose of the plane is pulled up sharply at the same time

Pin-bundle   A cluster of safety pins for bombs and missiles removed before takeoff, wrapped and stowed in the plane

Port Call   A date assigned by orders for a Marine to leave the U.S. or return

Press   Push the airplane beyond the normal release point

Punch Out   Eject from the plane

Quarter-roll   Put the wings of the plane 45 degrees from level flight

Race-track pattern   A long oval-shaped flight path, usually miles-long on the parallel sides

Radar Homing and Warning Gear, **RHAW**   Black boxes in the plane, wired into the pilot's and RIO's helmets, that let the aircrew know they are being watched or targeted by enemy radar

Ready room   Location where flight briefing and de-briefings take place

Red ink/black ink   Designation in flight log books indicating a combat hop (red ink) or non-combat (black ink)

Red Rocket   Designator for a highly important Naval message

Replacement Air Group, **RAG**   Training group for the tactical plane to which a Marine was assigned

RIO   Radio Intercept Officer, backseater in the Phantom

Appendix B

Rubber lady Military-issue air-mattress, coffin-shaped

Rules of Engagement Policy for conduct of military operations

Seabees Naval construction battalions, builders

Section / Lead / Two / Dash-Two / Wingman A group of two aircraft: the flight leader (Lead) and the wingman (Two or Dash-two)

Scope RIO

Senior officers Commissioned officers, majors and above

***Ships loading characteristics pamphlets,* SLCPs** Paperwork showing deck space, cranes, and storage holds in square- and cubic-feet for a military cargo ship

Shit-can Get rid of

Shit-hot A party suit, informal formal attire in Nam Phong, or as an adjective meaning *very good*

***Shitty Little Jobs Officer,* SLJO** Newest first lieutenant who became responsible for low-level jobs, e.g., making coffee

Sidewinder A heat-seeking air-to-air missile

Six-by A military truck with six wheels

Skipper Commanding Officer

Snake-eye bombs 500-pound bombs that popped out four fan-like fins upon release to retard the time of fall, usually used on low-level attacks

Sparrow A radar-beam-riding missile capable of destruction at significant stand-off distance

Stabilized A position in aerial refueling when the fighter is right behind the KC-130 and ready to plug in to the KC-130 basket

Status of forces agreement A formal agreement drawn by a host government for countries conducting combat or friendly operations based in the host country

Stick Pilot; or rows of loaded pallets about to be placed on a cargo airplane

***Surface-to-Air missile,* SAM** A lethal radar or ballistically aimed missile of varying size launched from the ground to destroy aircraft or other missiles

Glossary of Terms

Tailhook   Device that allows an aircraft to make an arrested landing, usually on a ship, by engaging the tailhook to a cross-deck cable. The stop is immediate and violent.

Tally-ho   Code talk for *I visually see the target/wingman/bogey, etc.*

Tanking   Aerial refueling

Temporary Additional Duty, TAD**, orders**   Doing a job without being sent to a permanent change of station for specified or unspecified lengths of time

Ten-degree run   A low-angle bomb run

Tin-benders   Metal smiths

Triple-A   Anti-aircraft artillery fire from large gun

Valsalva maneuver   Technique of attempted forced exhalation while the breath is held, used by aircrew in high-G loads

Vector   A direction in heading given toward an enemy

VMFA   Fixed-Wing Marine Fighter Attack. No one in the whole Marine Corps knows where the V came from.

Warrant   A document issued by the Secretary of the Navy designating a highly specialized and skilled person as a warrant officer. Lower than a commissioned officer, higher than enlisted ranks

Water buffalo   A wheel-mounted 600-gallon tank of potable water; or an animal native to Southeast Asia

Wes-Pac   Navy-speak for Western Pacific, at the time synonymous with Vietnam

Willie Pete   A White-Phosphorus smoke rocket used for marking targets

Winchester   Airplane code for *no ordnance* or ammunition

World   The United States

Zulu   Greenwich Mean Time, used by the military to coordinate movements worldwide by means of adding or subtracting the number of hours away the user is from the prime meridian

Zuni pack   A pack of five-inch-diameter forward-firing rockets for air-to-ground attack and Triple-A suppression

Appendix C:
Marine Corps Ranks

The following is a simplified representation of the ranks within the United States Marine Corps. For more detailed information, see https://www.marines.mil/Ranks/.

The United States Marine Corps includes three groups of officers: commissioned officers, warrant officers, and noncommissioned officers. Junior enlisted Marines form the bulk of the Corps but are not officers. Within each group, ranks are listed from highest to lowest.

Commissioned Officers: Most commissioned officers are college graduates, but not all of them. There are programs such as the Enlisted Commissioning Program, ECP, aka Bootstrap, whereby stellar enlisted men could earn a commission. There are also battlefield commissions, which have not been used since Vietnam. Commissioned officers have earned and accepted an appointment issued in the name of the President of the United States, giving them the responsibility to lead Marines as they defend the Constitution.

General Officers
(also Heavies, but rarely referred to that way in deference to their high rank)

General (4-stars)
Lieutenant General (3-stars)
Major General (2-stars)
Brigadier General (1-star)

Field Grade Officers
(commonly referred to as Heavies)

Colonel
Lieutenant Colonel
Major

Marine Corps Ranks

Company Grade
(junior officers)

Captain

First Lieutenant

Second Lieutenant

Warrant officers are specialists in what they do. They rate a salute from any enlisted man but cannot hold a command. They are officers by virtue of a warrant letter from the Secretary of the Navy recognizing their expertise and performance. Warrants cannot stand the duty watches because they are not unrestricted officers of the line, able to take over as a CO if necessary.

Chief Warrant Officer 5

Chief Warrant Officer 4

Chief Warrant Officer 3

Chief Warrant Officer 2

Warrant Officer

Noncommissioned officers (NCOs)
and Staff NCOs (longer-serving)

The Sergeant Major of the Marine Corps is the senior enlisted Marine, personally selected by the Commandant.

Staff NCO ranks include master gunnery sergeant/ sergeant major, master sergeant/first sergeant, gunnery sergeant and staff sergeant.

NCO ranks include corporal and sergeant.

Enlisted Marines include the ranks of lance corporal, private first class and private. They form the bulk of the Marine Corps.

Appendix D:
Brief Timeline
of the Vietnam War
(with personal notations
regarding the author's tour)

Circa 1954 President Eisenhower sent military personnel to South Vietnam to help the French.

1954 Ho Chi Minh's forces defeated the French at Dien Bien Phu.

1962 President Kennedy sent clandestine U.S. military to South Vietnam to stem communist aggression.

1965 President Johnson sent U.S. military, including Marines, to make the first landing at Da Nang, South Vietnam.

Late 1960s Royal Thai Air Force Base, Nam Phong, Thailand, aka The Rose Garden, was established on the site of a former CIA base.

1965–1973 North Vietnamese steadily moved south into South Vietnam, using Laos and Cambodia as infiltration routes, while the U.S. military defended the South Vietnamese.

1968 During the January lunar new year holiday, known as *Tet*, the North Vietnamese began a coordinated attack against South Vietnamese targets. U.S. and South Vietnamese forces suffered heavy losses, contributing to negative public opinion in the States about the war in Vietnam.

1968–1975 Refugees, generically referred to as *boat people*, fled Vietnam, Cambodia and Laos.

09/1972 First Lieutenant Fleet Lentz arrived at The Rose Garden.

Brief Timeline of the Vietnam War

12/1972   The *Christmas Bombings* of North Vietnam began in an attempt to get American POWs out and bring North Vietnam to the negotiating table in Paris.

1973   Serious negotiations began. As of January 23, 1973, the war in Vietnam was officially over. Before January 1973, all ground Marines had left Vietnam. Bombing in Laos and Cambodia continued until August.

03/1973   Lieutenant Lentz had his tour split and was re-assigned from squadron to group responsibilities, from VMFA-115 to MAG-15. He continued to fly combat hops while acting as *embarkation officer* and *scrounger.*

08/14/1973   Lieutenant Fleet Lentz flew his last combat hop.

08/1973   Order to activate *Operation Sunset,* the retrograde from RTAFB Nam Phong, The Rose Garden. U.S. Marines left The Rose Garden because bombing in Laos and Cambodia was stopped. MAG-15 was the last major Marine aviation command serving in combat in Southeast Asia and was ordered out in August.

09/1973   Lieutenant Lentz left Southeast Asia and returned to the world.

1975   North Vietnamese took Saigon. All U.S. personnel moved out of South Vietnam.

Appendix E:
Brief History of VMFA-115,
the Silver Eagles

VMFA-115 1972–1973 Silver Eagles Cruise Book includes a document entitled "The History of the Silver Eagles." The following information was excerpted from that document.

1943 VMF-115 was first organized and commissioned July 1, 1943, in Santa Barbara, Calif. Sixteen days later the squadron was turned over to the command of then Major Joe Foss, who went on to become the holder of the Marine World War Two record for number of enemy aircraft shot down—26. Foss was one of the most famous aces the Marine Corps produced. He later served as a U.S. Senator. Maybe he was not as notorious as Pappy Boyington but he was famous in his own right.

1944 The squadron was transferred to the Pacific campaign. A VMF-115 aircraft was the first to sink a Japanese submarine by employing a skip-bombing tactic from a Corsair propeller-driven fighter bomber. But keeping the airspace secure was the primary mission. After World War II, the squadron was transferred to (now) Beijing, China, to stand watch over U.S. interests should the communists attack. From there, the squadron moved to Hawaii and on to North Carolina, where it was the first Marine fighter squadron to receive a full complement of new F-9F Panther jet aircraft.

1950 VMF-115 became the first Marine fighter squadron to serve aboard an aircraft carrier, the USS *Roosevelt.*

1951 VMF-115 transferred to Pohang, Korea. From there 115 flew 9,250 combat sorties in 15,350 hours of combat flying. After Korea, the squadron transferred to MCAS El Toro, Calif., and changed airplanes to the F-4D Skyray, also known as *The Ford*. The squadron was also re-designated VMF (AW)-115, all weather. It was later reassigned to Atsugi, Japan, with defensive time in the Formosa Straits crisis.

1959   Squadron was shuttled back and forth between Atsugi, Japan, and Cherry Point, N.C.

1961   VMF-115 was assigned to MAG-24, 2nd Marine Aircraft Wing at MCAS Cherry Point, N.C.

1964   The squadron was re-designated VMFA-115 and transitioned to the Mach II F-4B Phantom II.

1965   The Silver Eagles were sent to Da Nang, Vietnam, and were in combat for most of the time during the Vietnam conflict.

1971–1972   Time-outs at Iwakuni, Japan. In April 1972, the squadron was sent back to Da Nang, Vietnam. In June 1972, the squadron was re-located to RTAFB, familiarly known as *The Rose Garden*. While there, the squadron topped 33,000 combat sorties in the Southeast Asia conflict, all theaters, more than any other Marine F-4 squadron, and received the Robert M. Hanson Award for fiscal year 1972 as the best Fighter Squadron in the Marine Corps.

1973   VMFA-115 left The Rose Garden.

Appendix F:
The Rose Garden's Legacy
of Leadership

To the best of my knowledge, The Rose Garden's legacy of leadership through men who eventually became General Officers has never been compiled.

Charlie Bolden, callsign Panther, of VA (AW)-533, was a hootch neighbor of mine in The Rose Garden. He earned a Distinguished Flying Cross and retired from the Marines as a two-star (major general). Panther later spent 14 years as an astronaut, flying 680 hours in space during four space shuttle missions, twice as commander and twice as pilot. He later became the administrator of NASA. https://www.nasa.gov/about/highlights/bolden_bio.html

Four men from VMFA-115 stationed at The Rose Garden in 1972–1973 later evolved past their ranks in that year to the status of General Officers. For four men out of the same outfit and stationed at the same location for such a short period of time to attain General rank is uncommon.

J. D. Howell, callsign Beak, became VMFA-115's only three-star (lieutenant general). Beak is featured in several chapters of this book and remains a friend. After 37 years as a Marine, Beak served as director of the Johnson Space Center, overseeing the Center's programs, including the space shuttle and International Space Station. He also oversaw spacecraft engineering and design, flight crew training, space and life sciences research and mission operations. http://www.epnaao.com/BIOS_files/REGULARS/Howell%20 Jefferson%20Davis%20(1).pdf

The Rose Garden's most distinguished legacy is not from the aviation side, so there is no callsign for Peter Pace, who went on to become a four-star general and the sixteenth Chairman of the Joint Chiefs of Staff, the first Marine to hold that position. In Nam Phong, Pete was XO of 3/9, the infantry security detachment. When we embarked out of The Rose Garden in 1973, grunt embarkation duties fell on his shoulders and I coordinated with him in my role as group embarkation officer. I would have been nicer to him, if I had known he would rise to Chairman, JCS. https://www.jcs.mil/About/The-Joint-Staff/Chairman/General-Peter-Pace/

Appendix G:
Suggested Reading
and Viewing

Bradley, Douglas and Craig Werner. *We Gotta Get Outta This Place.* Amherst: University of Massachusetts Press, 2015.

Burns, Ken, and Lynn Novick. *The Vietnam War, A Documentary by Ken Burns and Lynn Novick.* Public Television series. Directed by Ken Burns and Lynn Novick. Arlington, VA: PBS, 2017.

Marlantes, Karl. *Matterhorn: A Novel of the Vietnam War.* New York: Atlantic Monthly Press, 2010.

Mattis, Jim, and Bing West. *Call Sign-Chaos: Learning to Lead.* New York: Random House, 2019.

O'Brien, Tim. *The Things They Carried.* Boston: Houghton Mifflin Harcourt, 1990.

Pedersen, Dan. *Top Gun: An American Story.* New York: Hachette Books, 2019.

Petersen, Frank E., with J. Alfred Phelps. *Into the Tiger's Jaw: America's First Black Marine Aviator, The Autobiography of Lt. Gen. Frank E. Petersen.* Annapolis, MD: Naval Institute Press, 2012.

Sledge, E.B. *With the Old Breed: At Peleliu and Okinawa.* New York: Oxford University Press, 1990.

Webb, James. *Fields of Fire.* Annapolis, Md.: Naval Institute Press, 1978.

Appendix H:
Brief Career Overview

Fleet S. Lentz, Jr., Col, USMCR (Ret), was commissioned as a Second Lieutenant in the United States Marine Corps in 1969 and received his wings as a Naval Flight Officer in 1971. Assigned to the Western Pacific, Lentz served in the Vietnam conflict in 1972–1973, flying 131 combat missions in the F-4B Phantom II, out of Nam Phong, Thailand, and Da Nang, Republic of Vietnam. After the war, Lentz served as executive officer of VMFA-112 and commanding officer of Headquarters and Maintenance Squadron/Marine Aviation Logistics 41, both based at Navy Dallas. He attended Navy Fighter Weapons School (Top Gun) in 1982. Lentz retired from the Marine Corps in 2000 with 31 years of affiliated time and 1500+ hours in the F-4.

He also worked for 32 years in civilian commercial aviation at the management and executive levels, including 20 years as North American Vice President of Volvo Aero, headquarters in Bromma, Sweden. He lives in Centennial, Colorado.

Index

Numbers in **bold** italics indicate pages with illustrations

Index

Index

Index